MW01444888

Praise for *The Savvy Working Mom*

"*The Savvy Working Mom* is a must-read for mothers striving to create a life they love. Whitnee Hawthorne's wisdom is both practical and inspiring, and she offers tools that truly work for real moms with real lives."

JILL KOZIOL, cofounder and former CEO of Motherly
and coauthor of *The Motherly Guide to Becoming Mama*

―✦―

"Insightful, practical, and deeply empowering, *The Savvy Working Mom* is the ultimate guide for moms navigating the demands of career and family. Whitnee Hawthorne's wisdom is transformative—this book is a must-read for any mom ready to thrive!"

KATYA LIBIN, cofounder of HeyMama

―✦―

"As a former executive and a mom, I wish I'd had this book earlier in my career. Whitnee Hawthorne brilliantly tackles the myth of work-life balance and offers practical strategies to help women thrive both at work and at home."

JENNIFER "JEN" KEM, CEO of Master Brand Institute
and author of *Unicorn Team*

"This book captures the emotions I felt throughout my thirty-year career in the corporate world. As a single mom of two and a senior leader of a multi-billion-dollar company, I know how it feels to pursue the holy grail called work-life balance—frustrating and elusive. I'm glad Whitnee Hawthorne is lifting the veil and setting women free from the ridiculous idea that to be considered a success, we must do it all. *The Savvy Working Mom* reminds us that true success and happiness are found when we decide to do what matters most."

PAM NEMEC, CEO of Pam Nemec Consulting, Inc., and leadership and communication keynote speaker

---

"I worked with Whitnee Hawthorne and was always in awe of her accomplishments, energy, and confidence. As an executive and working mom of three daughters myself, I can tell you that Whitnee's 7 Ds of successful delegation are game changers."

MEAGEN EISENBERG, CMO of Samsara

A Guide to Prioritization, Delegation, and Making Time for Cocktails

THE SAVVY WORKING MOM

WHITNEE HAWTHORNE

PAGE TWO

Copyright © 2025 by Whitnee Hawthorne

All rights reserved. No part of this book may be reproduced, stored in a retrieval system or transmitted, in any form or by any means, without the prior written consent of the publisher or a license from The Canadian Copyright Licensing Agency (Access Copyright). For a copyright license, visit accesscopyright.ca or call toll free to 1-800-893-5777.

This book is not intended as a substitute for consultation with a healthcare professional. Please consult with your own physician or healthcare specialist regarding the suggestions and recommendations made in this book.

Cataloguing in publication information is available from Library and Archives Canada.
ISBN 978-1-77458-519-1 (flexiback)
ISBN 978-1-77458-520-7 (ebook)

Page Two
pagetwo.com

Cover design by Taysia Louie
Interior design by Fiona Lee
Printed and bound in Canada by Friesens
Distributed in Canada by Raincoast Books
Distributed in the US and internationally by Macmillan

25 26 27 28 29   5 4 3 2 1

thesavvyworkingmom.com

*To all the working mamas out there—
this is for you and your kids.*

Contents

The Savvy Working Mom's Manifesto 1

Introduction: Pause, Take a Beat, Take a Breath, I Got You 3

1 **Moving Past Work-Life Balance** 9
2 **Releasing the Idea of Doing It All** 21
3 **The Art of Saying No with Love and without Guilt** 31
4 **The 7 Ds of Successful Delegation** 39
5 **Busting the Myths That Keep Us from Delegating** 49
6 **Determine: Assess Tasks and Decide What to Delegate** 59
7 **Define: Specify What Success Looks Like** 71
8 **Decide Who: Select the Right People Based on Skills and Capacity** 79

9   **Do the Math: Figure Out the Time Required to Teach What You Need** *89*

10 **Discuss: Clearly Communicate the Task, Expectations, and Deadlines** *97*

11 **Discourse: Follow Up, Provide Guidance, and Evaluate Progress** *119*

12 **(Happy) Dance: Celebrate Your Win!** *131*

13 **Staying on the Prioritization and Delegation Path** *137*

14 **The Grace and Joy Morning Routine** *149*

15 **The Next Moment** *165*

Extra, Extra: How to Do It *171*

Acknowledgments *209*

The Savvy Working Mom's Manifesto

I take care of myself first. I need my light so I can light a path for those I love.

I am honest. I share what's on my mind and in my heart. The good, the bad, the ugly. My authentic story is an inspiration.

I never try to do it all. I do only the things that matter to make my dreams come true.

I am kind to myself. Perfection is neither my goal nor my destination.

I enjoy the ride. Motherhood is a journey with my children.

I am present. I put my phone down and live in the moment wherever I am.

I am brave. I let go of social pressure and do what is right for me and my family.

I lend a hand. I pull others up with me as I rise.

I believe in myself. I am capable of changing the world and living a life I love.

I deserve all the love and light. My dreams are worthy, and I deserve to have them come true.

_# Introduction:
Pause, Take a Beat, Take a Breath, I Got You

OH, THE ALLURING promise of work-life balance—a concept that's been dangled in front of us like a golden key that will unlock the secret door to all our hopes and dreams. But what if this pursuit of balance was just a wild-goose chase from the get-go? What if, instead of being the answer, work-life balance is part of the problem?

We rely on the promise of finally finding peace, joy, and fulfillment if we could only become the woman on the poster we have in our mind's eye, the woman who seems to effortlessly balance it all. We count on the benefits of climbing the career ladder while rocking flawless makeup at school drop-offs, nailing the perfect parent act, being the ultimate BFF, and playing the role of the ideal spouse, while shining like a superstar in our community.

What if this relentless pursuit is what's actually stealing our peace? Could trying to emulate our imaginary perfect woman be the very thing that's making us feel unfulfilled?

What if aspiring to be that woman is actually diminishing our value and undercutting our worth?

We live in a world that was not designed for working moms. These promises are like houses built on sand, and they're setting us up for despair, sadness, and failure.

Mama, if you're feeling overwhelmed, exhausted, frustrated, or just plain tired, I got you.

If you feel like it's all hanging by a thread, and you're afraid to find out what happens when everything falls apart, I got you.

If you worry that you can't be the mom you want to be, the "you" you want to be and grow your career, I got you.

If you know doing it all is going to be the death of you and your situation isn't sustainable, I got you.

Work-life balance is a myth.

Doing it all is likely robbing you of joy, holding you back from peace, and leaving you unfulfilled and overwhelmed.

Together, we are going to move past work-life balance, ditch overwhelm, release the unhelpful (and maybe masochistic) practice of doing it all, and ultimately find the peace you rightfully deserve. We're going to do this by learning how to strategically prioritize, eliminate, and delegate responsibilities, because the secret to flourishing as a working mama is determined by what you *don't* do. One more time, for the cheap seats in the back (and in case you are skimming):

The secret to flourishing as a working mama is determined by what you *don't* do.

We'll even make enough time to leisurely enjoy a cocktail along the way. Sound good?

YOU ARE AMAZING. You have everything you need to live a fulfilling life that you love while being at peace. You can be the mom, the you, and the career woman you want to be, and I will show you how.

The secret to flourishing
as a working mama
is determined by what
you *don't* do.

First, let me peel back the layers of the work-life balance sham and expose how it sets us up for failure in not one but several eye-roll-worthy ways.

Here's how I came to realize that this whole work-life balance thing is nothing more than a silly charade society has orchestrated, designed to set us up for failure.

Picture this: I'd just returned to work after a four-month maternity leave. My boss, husband, friends, and even my team were all incredibly supportive. Still, being a working woman and a devoted mom was a tough juggling act.

One day, I found myself in a situation. I had to pick up my little bundle of joy from day care, and work, as it often does, was running late. I was living in Brooklyn at the time, and our day care had this policy: if you're late, they hit you with a fine of one dollar per minute for the first half hour. And if you manage to stretch your lateness beyond that, well, congratulations, your kid gets a one-way ticket to the police precinct! I know it sounds like day care boot camp, but it's what we agreed to when we signed on the dotted line.

So there I was, my last call was running over, and I was now running late to pick up my son. So, I hatched a genius plan. I'd finish my call on the train ride home, multitasking like a pro. I strolled out of the office, earbud in place, and pressed on with my call while waiting for the train. The train arrived, I hopped on, and everything seemed manageable despite the tight schedule. I was engrossed in my call, making a crucial point, when the train screeched to a halt.

"Ladies and gentlemen, we've got a signal malfunction," the conductor announced. "We'll be on our way shortly."

A minor inconvenience, I thought. I still had time left.

But then, the unimaginable happened. My call dropped precisely as we entered a network dead zone. One minute passed, and I felt a tad anxious; two minutes, and I was a bundle of nerves. The conductor returned with another dreaded announcement.

"Folks, we're in for an extended delay."

Panic set in, and I started trying to push through the train to get a signal. Time was slipping away, and I was on the verge of missing the day care pickup. Could they really take my son to the precinct? I couldn't reach the day care because, you guessed it, dead zone. Colleagues probably thought I was wholly unprofessional and had ghosted them on the call. My husband was unreachable, thanks to that same dead zone. Disappointment loomed large. I was failing as a mom, as a wife, as a colleague, and most importantly, I was failing myself. Tears welled up, and there I was, crying my heart out on the train. In public.

Embarrassment crept in—first, because of my public meltdown, and second, because I was crumbling under the weight of the so-called work-life balance. I had all the support, all the flexibility, and yet I couldn't make it work. It had never been this hard before. Why couldn't I just figure out how to balance work and life?

Out of that embarrassment grew an inferno of anger. I was mad. Furious even. Mad because I realized that I'd been sold a bill of goods gone bad. Furious because this idea of work-life balance was a load of malarkey, a setup for failure, and it wasn't just me. It was setting up all working mothers for the same fall.

At that moment, I made a promise to myself—no more nonsense. No more falling for the work-life balance trap. I vowed to find a better way. And, miraculously, the train started moving again. I got to my son before they could haul him off to jail. (And to this day, I'm not sure if they've ever sent a baby to the clink.)

From that point on, I embarked on a journey of discovery. I worked with and interviewed countless working moms from every career stage, determined to unearth an alternative to the elusive balance.

Guess what? I found it. I not only found it but also applied it to my own life, and let me tell you, I've been living in pure joy ever since. At work, I even managed to leap from a director role to vice president (while expecting my second son) and soared all the way to the C-suite before my eldest turned five.

The keys to my success that have been the most effective include releasing the idea of doing it all, ruthlessly prioritizing, strategically delegating, and making time for a cocktail or two.

The rest of this book is my treasure trove of secrets, tips, and tricks—all designed to help you flourish, not just at home and work but everywhere in between.

It's time to ditch the work-life balance myth and step into a world where you can truly thrive.

1

Moving Past Work-Life Balance

Ever hear something that flips your whole world upside down? Yeah, that happened to me too, and I'm about to drop that same bomb on you with a quote that'll make you rethink everything. But before we dive into that, let me paint you a picture of the old me.

Pre-kids, I was the quintessential yes-woman. Not the brownnosing type, mind you, but the one who couldn't resist saying yes to every project, every favor, every freakin' thing that came my way. Need help with that office shindig? Count me in. Hate the idea of chatting with that vendor? I'll take one for the team and sit in on that meeting. Need someone to burn the midnight oil to finish that report? No sweat, I'll sacrifice happy hour. Need an early bird to catch the worm for that meeting setup? Consider it done. Day or night, rain or shine, I was your go-to gal.

Being the yes-woman had its perks, no doubt. It boosted my career, giving me exposure, which garnered influence. It showed folks I was reliable and dependable—the whole nine yards. Plus, it landed me in meetings where I could soak up wisdom like a sponge, learning the ropes from the bigwigs and applying this knowledge to my own teams.

But let's be real: it also sucked up a ton of my time. Back then, I didn't mind. I was young, fit, and fueled by quad espressos. So what if I couldn't stay out late because I had an early morning grind? I could be home by 1:00 a.m. and wake up at 6:00 a.m.; I still got my dose of fun. Maybe I couldn't sleep until noon on a Saturday so that I could finish a report before trotting off to brunch. That's ok, who needs sleep anyway? Honestly, for a while I thrived like that. Feeling needed at work, having a robust social life, going to the gym most mornings, and gallivanting around the city most nights.

Then, I had a baby. And just like that, everything changed.

The script was flipped. I always knew I would go back to work. And once I was back, I quickly realized the way I was living, and how I was delivering value at work, simply wasn't sustainable. Those late nights, early mornings, and weekends going the extra mile were no longer an option. I had a four-month-old at home who required all of that time and more. And for some reason, staying up all night with a four-month-old is not as invigorating as clubbing all night—it's just exhausting. My energy was at an all-time low, and my responsibilities felt like they were at an all-time high.

And here is where it gets interesting.

Remember that story where I was crying on the train? Not too long after that I was listening to a podcast episode that mentioned a quote from Sean Covey: "Saying 'yes' to one thing means saying 'no' to another."

It sucker-punched me. That message, and what it meant in the context of my career, almost knocked me out.

- Saying yes to a fluff vendor meeting means saying no to supporting a team member.
- Saying yes to running that extra report means saying no to using that time for strategic planning or brainstorming.
- Saying yes to constantly checking emails means saying no to deep, focused work that requires concentration.
- Saying yes to every client request means saying no to dedicating time for skills development or training.
- Saying yes to attending every networking event means saying no to the sleep needed to make good decisions.
- Saying yes to frequent overtime means saying no to recuperating.
- Saying yes to attending every team-building activity means saying no to focused project work.
- Saying yes to accepting every meeting invitation means saying no to getting project work done during a workday.

And this wasn't just at work; it was at home too.

- Saying yes to cleaning the house means saying no to spending quality time with your family.
- Saying yes to cooking a complicated meal means saying no to relaxing and unwinding after a long day.
- Saying yes to running errands means saying no to enjoying a leisurely afternoon at home.

- Saying yes to organizing clutter means saying no to pursuing a hobby or personal interest.
- Saying yes to helping a friend move means saying no to having a quiet weekend to recharge.
- Saying yes to brunch means saying no to getting some extra rest.
- Saying yes to tackling home improvement projects means saying no to indulging in self-care activities.

Balance, my foot

Let's start by debunking the big whopper of a myth: that work-life balance is all about divvying up our precious time between the nine-to-five grind and the rest of our so-called life. It sounds like a simple math problem. Spoiler alert: it's anything but.

So, we've got 168 hours in a week, right? A full-time job eats up at least forty of those hours, give or take, and that's before factoring in the commute, overtime, and the time spent just thinking about work when you should be off the clock. Let's say you spend an hour commuting to and from work, that's another ten hours. And, like a good girl, you are prioritizing sleep (more on this in another chapter), so you are getting eight hours of sleep each night. That's fifty-six hours of your week to get the rest your body requires. Put it all together and you are spending an easy 106 out of the 168 hours you have in a week on work and sleep. This leaves a measly sixty-two hours for living your life.

Not much balance there. This time-management charade of work-life balance leaves us chasing our tails, desperately trying to catch an ideal that's about as elusive as a unicorn in the wild.

Don't limit your life to
balancing on a tightrope;
acknowledge it for
the symphony it is.

Life is more than work versus everything else

Next up, let's talk about how the work-life balance myth crams our complex lives into just two boxes: work and everything that's not work. "Life" isn't just some lump of stuff to balance against work. I've identified nine areas of life for a working mom. Given that the importance of each area as it relates to another can change over time (even from day to day), here are they are listed in no specific order.

1. *Career/work:* It's how you earn your living, whether you're climbing the corporate ladder, freelancing, or running your empire.

2. *Relationship with kids:* It's who you are to your children and how you spend your time and energy with them.

3. *Health:* This is your whole health—both physical and mental.

4. *Relationship with partner, self, or if you're single and ready to mingle... dating:* Whether you're nurturing the flame with your partner, enjoying a hot date with yourself, or diving back into the dating pool, your personal relationships are important.

5. *Finances:* This is how financially secure you are.

6. *Personal growth:* Personal growth isn't a luxury; it's a necessity. It's about nurturing your mind, chasing your passions, and evolving into the most fabulous version of yourself.

7. *Fun and adventure:* Fun and adventure are about the things you do to bring joy into your life.

8. *Physical environment:* These are the spaces where you spend time, including your home, or, if you commute a lot like I do, your car or office space.

9 *Community and giving back:* This is about connecting with others, making a difference, and spreading a little love and kindness.

The idea of trying to balance one area equally against the other eight simply isn't possible. It basically leaves you spending your life trying to make a dollar outta fifteen cents.

Your life is dynamic, like a symphony, not static, like a tightrope

The idea of work-life balance asks us to separate work and life as if they are not fully intertwined. When we try to balance work against "life," we're missing the point entirely. We're ignoring the fact that a fulfilling career can boost our personal lives, just as personal growth can supercharge our professional game. Our lives can't be neatly compartmentalized into hours dedicated to work and hours reserved for "life."

The best analogy I've found is to think of our full lives, all nine areas, as a beautiful piece of music in a symphony. You need every instrument for it to sound complete. You need every area of life to live fulfilled. At different times, specific areas of your life will require more of your time and energy. Sometimes these will come in the form of a solo act; other times there will be duets and trios. Ultimately, all the areas fold back into the music to complete the piece.

I have a four-year-old, a six-year-old, a husband, a job, and a side hustle. All of these are important to me, and each commitment needs something from me. You can guess that each and every day there are changes in what and how much is needed on all fronts. When I thought about balancing those needs, I would imagine myself as a tightrope walker, with one of those long poles that have weights on either side. One of the weights was "work" and the other was "life." Guess what? They never ever weighed the same, and I was always toppling off that stupid tightrope.

Now, knowing that my life is dynamic and vibrant, and there are nine areas, I like to think of it more like a symphony. Some days, work plays a solo; on other days, my kids do. Still on other days, there are duets between my side hustle and my husband. Like a complicated piece of music, my life is dynamic; it's constantly flowing, and it is beautiful. So is yours. Don't limit your life to balancing on a tightrope; acknowledge it for the symphony it is.

In conclusion, the myth of perfect balance is just that—a myth. It's an unattainable ideal that has us chasing unicorns instead of living our lives authentically. Life is messy, dynamic, and ever-changing, and that's what makes it beautiful. Instead of striving for perfection, let's embrace the imperfections, ride the waves of life, and find our own unique rhythm. It's time to let go of the unicorn chase and start living a life that's real, imperfect, and wonderfully yours.

So, here's the mic-drop moment: the work-life balance illusion, though well intentioned, is nothing more than smoke and mirrors.

Instead of striving for an unattainable equilibrium, let's shift our focus to a more holistic view of life. One that embraces the beautiful chaos of our experiences and lets us flourish in every aspect of our existence.

It's time to break free from the shackles of an idea that has us running in circles and start living our lives in all their messy, glorious splendor.

When I ditched the idea of work-life balance, I realized I needed to start saying no a lot more if I wanted to say yes to the things that would move the needle for me.

It's time to ditch the idea of work-life balance and embrace the symphony of our lives.

So, I got really clear on what was most important to me:

- Kicking my career into high gear, making a mark at the office, and, let's not forget, fattening up that paycheck (because diapers and baby food aren't cheap)
- Savoring quality time with my family
- Leaving a little room for me

Once I knew what I wanted, I took four steps to make my dreams a reality.

1. I set serious goals in each area.
2. I set boundaries.
3. I revamped the processes and systems I was using at home, at work, and everywhere else.
4. I leaned into prioritization and delegation.

Embrace the symphony of your life

So, Mama, now you are in on the little secret that's been whispered about in the corridors of corporate boardrooms and living room playdates. It's time to ditch the idea of work-life balance and embrace the symphony of our lives. We're about to embark on a journey of unapologetically embracing a new perspective—one that's all about living life to the fullest without the pressure of perfect balance.

Let's celebrate harmony over balance. Let's allow the various facets of our lives to coexist, to intertwine, and to complement each other.

Imagine this: Your career fuels your passion, and your personal growth enhances your performance at work. Your family becomes your support system, and your health and well-being are your secret weapons for success. Living in harmony means you're not juggling separate balls; you're conducting a symphony where every instrument plays a vital role. Living in harmony brings peace.

By adopting this perspective, you're no longer held hostage by the quest for perfect balance. You're free to prioritize what matters in the moment, whether it's a project deadline, a family dinner, or self-care.

It's time to toss that tightrope of work-life balance into the circus tent and embrace a new perspective—one that celebrates the beautiful symphony of life. It's time to trade balance and tightropes for a fabulous life that's uniquely yours. Embrace it, live it, and sashay through life like the fabulous star you are!

Cheers to moving past the idea of work-life balance!

Congrats, Mama! I'm so proud that you have made it this far. Yes, I know we are still at the beginning of this process, but I also know you have a lot going on. I'm proud that you are making the time to read this and make space for a new way of living, one that will give you peace.

Moving past the idea of work-life balance, something you've been told is the answer to your overwhelm for your entire life, is not easy. I've given you a lot to think about. So, you know what I like to do when I have a lot to think about? I like to make myself something pretty to drink, sit on my porch with a journal, sip that pretty drink, stare into space, sip, process, write, and repeat until I feel the idea settling in me.

To that end, I'm going to share with you a recipe for one of my favorite pretty sippers, the Jackée Rose. This cocktail is based on the Jack Rose, which originated during Prohibition and was popular in speakeasies. I've updated the recipe to replace grenadine with the juice from a jar of maraschino cherries, which is a fun flavor that always gives positive vibes. I named the cocktail Jackée after the actress who played the sassy and saucy Sandra on the TV show 227. I know I'm dating myself with that show, but listen, that character lived her life on her terms and was ready to tangle with anyone about social norms. Seems fitting, given I'm asking you to buck the work-life balance norm of our era.

JACKÉE ROSE

Ingredients

2 ounces applejack or apple brandy

¾ ounce fresh lemon juice

½ ounce maraschino cherry juice

Lemon peel or one maraschino cherry, for garnish (optional)

Instructions

1. Fill a cocktail shaker with ice cubes.
2. Add the applejack or apple brandy, lemon juice, and maraschino cherry juice to the shaker.
3. Shake well until the mixture is thoroughly chilled, about 15 to 20 seconds.
4. Strain the mixture into a chilled cocktail glass.
5. Optionally, garnish with a lemon peel or a maraschino cherry.
6. Serve and enjoy your refreshing Jackée Rose!

Note: Adjust the amount of cherry juice according to your taste for sweetness. You can also experiment with different types of apple brandy or applejack for variations in flavor.

2

Releasing the Idea of Doing It All

I REMEMBER A FEW DAYS after getting engaged to my now-husband, when I was lying in bed blissfully daydreaming about our future. Cue the fantasies of being the ultimate boss lady: married with two wonderful boys and a beautiful girl, rocking my career as a VP, and still finding time to slay in the volunteer game. I'm dropping my impeccably dressed kiddos off at school, strutting my stuff at work, and hitting up all the hot spots on weekends.

Life's a dream, right?

Fast-forward in time to after having our first baby. I remember dragging myself home from work one day, having picked up our son from day care. His socks were mismatched; I was exhausted and about fifteen pounds heavier than I wanted to be. I just got a text from a friend asking me to meet them for brunch in two weeks, and I knew I was going to say no. Even though I was tired, I started to make dinner, a sheet-pan meal, because day care in Brooklyn costs almost as much as our rent and with that came a tight budget. I slid the pan in the oven, sat slumped onto the sofa, looked at my son on the carpet, and thought, Man, I'm happy.

Then the oddest thing happened. I started to question my happiness. I'm happy, but wait, shouldn't I be striving for more?

Shouldn't I be a VP by now, hitting up fancy events, and keeping my Insta feed on fire?

Why am I content with this mismatched sock situation? My to-do list is as long as a CVS receipt and nowhere near complete.

Cue the internal monologue of self-doubt and comparison.

I really started going in on myself and making a list in my head of the ways I needed to improve and all the things I needed to do. I started to feel overwhelmed with everything I should be doing and wasn't. I started to feel frustrated for being so behind and sad because I was struggling to get it all done and I wasn't that superwoman on the poster. Even though moments ago I was happy.

Then like a ton of bricks, something I heard once on a TV show hit me: "Don't let comparison be the thief of joy."

I was comparing myself to the ideal image I had back before I was actually living this married, working-mom life. I was looking at the poster of the woman-who does-it-all and thinking I needed to do that, to be her, to be happy. Even though, at that moment, I was *actually* happy.

I was letting all the things I thought I should be stop me from enjoying who I was.

Get "should" out of
your vocabulary.
There is no room for
"should" in your life.

So I said to myself, "Whitnee, don't 'should' on yourself! Why do you need to be all those things?"

And you know what? I didn't have an answer.

Don't should on yourself

So I made a list. (I love a list.) A good ol' list of all the shoulds cluttering up my brain:

- I should cook and serve a hot dinner every night.
- I should enroll my kid in music, baby soccer, and the Mommy and Me class.
- I should look fresh 24/7.
- I should say yes to any extra assignment offered at work.
- I should have a spotless house.
- I should be a museum regular.
- I should read a book a week.
- I should hit the gym five times a week.
- I should volunteer.
- I should start eating more cleanly.

Then I gave 'em the side-eye and asked myself three simple questions:

1. Do I actually want this, or is it just society, Instagram, or my mom in my ear?
2. Will this bring me joy? Like, legit happiness?
3. Is this gonna move the needle in my life or career? Like, am I gonna look back on this and say, "Yep, that was a game changer"?

And let me tell you, as I sifted through that list, I had a bit of an epiphany. There were things I needed to do—ya know, to keep the lights on and all that jazz. Then there were things that would make me happy, like really, genuinely happy. And let's not forget the stuff that was gonna set me up for a future brighter than the sun. But there were also things that, honestly, were just things to be doing.

So I took that list and gave it a makeover. I divided it into three categories:

1 Need to do—yep, these are non-negotiables, the gotta-get-it-done tasks.

2 Want to do—hello, happiness! These are the things that light my fire and make life worth livin'.

3 Should do, but nah—ah, the shoulds. They sound good on paper, but they're just not my jam.

For example:

I need to hustle at work—gotta pay those bills, am I right? I want to climb that career ladder, take on that extra project—gonna reach the top like a boss.

I should help with the office party, but let's be real, planning ain't my thing, and it ain't gonna land me that corner office.

And hey, dressing my kid for the weather? That's a must. Dressing him like a baby Instagram model? Not so much.

As for fashion, sure, I could go haute couture, but if I feel fly in Birkenstocks, who cares if they're not runway-worthy?

And reading more? Absolutely. Hitting up a museum? Eh, maybe. But only if it's gonna light my creative spark.

So there you have it—my revamped list. No more shoulds, just a whole lotta doin' what feels right.

Focus on what you need, what you want, and what truly lights your fire.

I decided I needed to release the shoulds. I needed to get "should" out of my vocabulary. I either needed to or wanted to do something. There was no room for "should" in my life. "Should" was the result of comparing my life to what others wanted for me. While others may have the best intentions for me, just because they think it's good for me doesn't mean it is. Just because society thinks I should be doing something doesn't mean that thing is actually going to help me or make me happy.

I took each "should" and slapped it on a bright Post-it note. With a nod of appreciation, I acknowledged their good intentions, but couldn't help but smirk at the irony—ain't it funny how the path to burnout is lined with well-meaning shoulds? So I gathered those little squares of obligation and tossed 'em into a bowl in the sink.

With a flick of the match, I watched those suckers go up in flames. As the fire danced and dwindled, a weight lifted off my shoulders. Goodbye, shoulds—hello, freedom! And as those literal Post-its turned to ashes, I symbolically torched that picture-perfect poster of the superwoman I thought I had to be.

In its place, I modernized the poster and made it a reel. I then embraced the reel of my ever-changing life, sprinkled with moments of pure joy. It was time to let go of the pressure to do it all and instead focus on what truly brought me happiness and fulfillment.

Now before we dive into the nitty-gritty of strategic delegation, let's take a moment to toss out the shoulds. Trust me, life's too short to live by someone else's checklist. Let's focus on what we need, what we want, and what truly lights our fire.

Activity

- Make a list of all the things you think you *should* be doing.
- Recategorize those shoulds into needs, wants, and shoulds.
- Burn (in a safe way) the shoulds.

Cheers to not should-ing on yourself!

Letting go of the shoulds? Honey, it's a roller coaster of emotions. One minute you're feeling relieved, like a weight's been lifted off your shoulders; the next, you're hit with a wave of nostalgia or maybe even a touch of sadness. But amidst all the feels, there's something undeniably empowering about it.

The day after I bid adieu to my shoulds, I felt like I could conquer the world. I was free to focus on what truly mattered to me, to set boundaries, and to redefine my own version of success. It was liberating, exhilarating even. It felt like cause for celebration.

And what better way to celebrate than with bubbles!

A Kir and a Kir Royale are both classic French cocktails, named after Félix Kir, a mayor of Dijon, France, who popularized them in the mid-twentieth century. Kir is made by mixing cassis and white wine. A Kir Royale is a bit fancier and made by mixing cassis with champagne (or any bubbles you have on hand).

Oddly enough, I had my first Kir Royale in Spain. One of my fabulous aunties took me with her and her husband on a trip to Spain for my high school graduation. I spoke Spanish, so it was a bit of a gift and a bit of free translation services.

One night we were at dinner in this super tiny and beautiful town. My aunt ordered a Kir Royale. Now I was not a high school drinker (I know, shocker), but when that drink came out with its beautiful cassis glow and tiny bubbles, I was entranced. I could not stop looking at it. She offered me a taste, and honestly, I was a bit afraid. Then she said, "You know it's legal to drink here when you're eighteen." And that was enough for me. I had a sip, and it actually tasted just as good as it looked. To my shock, she ordered me one. That was my first drink at a restaurant and to this day one of my favorite drinks for a celebration.

KIR ROYALE

Ingredients

½ ounce crème de cassis (black currant liqueur)

Champagne or sparkling wine

Fresh raspberry or blackberry, for garnish (optional)

Instructions

1. Pull out your favorite champagne glass, flute, or coupe, and add the crème de cassis.
2. Slowly pour the chilled champagne or sparkling wine into the glass, over the crème de cassis.
3. Gently stir the mixture with a cocktail stirrer or a long spoon to combine the flavors.
4. Optionally, garnish the glass with a fresh raspberry or blackberry.
5. Serve immediately and enjoy your Kir Royale!

Note: You can adjust the ratio of crème de cassis to champagne according to taste. If you prefer a sweeter drink, add a little more crème de cassis.

3

The Art of Saying No with Love and without Guilt

ALRIGHT, MAMA, you did not just go through all of that work to let your calendar fill up again. But it can happen so easily. I know; I've been there. I've ended a workday, looked at my to-do list, and it was longer than when I had started the day.

I don't know how it happened. It was just like from one day to the next, I suddenly had more to do than I could manage and overwhelm crept in. That's when I reminded myself about the importance of eliminating and delegating tasks.

Now I go through my list, eliminate things, delegate more, then get very focused on vetting every new task that comes my way.

Just a friendly reminder that trying to do it all will be your downfall. Doing it all is not the path to happiness or fulfillment. The way that trying to do it all made you feel is likely the reason you picked up this book in the first place.

So take a moment and reflect on your new reel, the one that you've put up with the woman you want to be. Picture her and all the amazing things she is doing. Revisit the list you created of the things that will move the needle and make your heart sing. Focus on those and remember that with each task that comes your way, saying yes also means saying no.

It can be hard to vet new tasks, but I've got a tool that can help. This tool can quickly help you figure out whether you should start a new task, and it applies to all areas of life. I call it the to-do or not-to-do checklist.

When something new comes your way, ask yourself these seven questions.

To-do or not-to-do checklist

1. Does it feel fun?
2. Does it give you an opportunity to grow?
3. Will it move you toward a life you love?
4. Is it aligned with your core values?
5. Is the opportunity cost worth the gain?
6. Do you have the capacity to execute this without depleting your spirit?
7. Does this excite or scare you?

If you don't answer six or seven of these questions with a yes, this task is probably something you'll want to pass on.

Now I understand that saying no is uncomfortable. It's so uncomfortable that we often say yes to things we don't even want to do to avoid the uncomfortable and inconvenient feelings that we have at the moment. So rather than put someone out, we put ourselves out by saying yes and committing our time and energy to things that stop us from being the woman we want to be.

This is not setting ourselves up to shine. This is taking away the time we could spend with our children, time we could spend on work that advances our careers, and time we could use to rest and recover.

We need to learn to say no in a polite and firm way.

- Saying no does not make you a bad person.
- Saying no does not make you a bad friend.
- Saying no makes you true to your own personal needs.
- Saying no frees you up to do the things that are most important in your life.

And your life does need to come first so that you can be the best you for everyone around you.

The following are various ways that you can say no to someone.

Remember, the most important thing about saying no is understanding that for you to say yes to what matters in your life, you're going to have to say no to other things. Be polite but firm, then keep it moving.

Just a friendly reminder that trying to do it all will be your downfall.

Ways to say no

- *No.* No is a full sentence. If you can, simply say no and leave it at that. It's not rude; it's just the truth.
- *No, thank you.* If you want to sweeten up your no, you can add thank you to the end of the sentence. "No, thank you" is polite and firm.
- *I'm not able to make it.* This is saying no in a way that clearly communicates you are unavailable. "I'm not able to make it" showcases that you would like to, but it is just not possible at this time. That is something that anyone should be able to understand.
- *I'm booked at that time.* This statement makes it clear that you already have another commitment. It also signals to the person who's asking you that if you were to do what they need, you would have to break your other commitments, and that is just a lot for them to ask of you and whoever else you're committed to.
- *Let me check my calendar.* This statement is not as firm, but if you are the type of person who is easing into the world of saying no, it is very convenient. "Let me check my calendar" gives you time and space to breathe. While I like to advocate speaking directly to someone when you have to decline something they've asked of you, it also gives you the space to email or text them back that you are now committed at the time they want you to do whatever it is they're asking.
- *As it turns out, I can't.* This is one of my favorite phrases. "As it turns out" eases the burn of no. "As it turns out, I can't" implies that there are other circumstances and things

going on in your life and in the world that are leading to your inability to participate. It is firm and polite and a little less harsh than a direct no.

- *I can't, but have you asked...?* I like this phrase because it helps to point the person who is asking something of you in another direction. You're clear and direct by saying that you can't do whatever it is that they're asking, but you are also offering to help by pointing them in the direction of someone who might be able to.

- *It's not possible, but have you tried...?* Similar to the above, with this phrase, you are firm and polite in declining your availability, yet you are offering up another alternative to the person who needs help.

- *Thanks for thinking of me, but I can't.* Here is another way to be firm but polite. If a straight no is too much for you, then you can simply say, "Thanks for thinking of me, but I can't." It shows gratitude, which is always positive, yet it gives a clear message that you are not available.

- *I'm honored, but I can't.* This is another way to show gratitude when someone asks you to do something, but it also clearly states that you are not available to help. Being honored says that you appreciate how they think of you and believe you could help them. You recognize that they believe you're capable and you appreciate it, yet you are also cognizant of your time and what's going on in your life and firmly state you're not available to help.

Just like delegating, learning to say no can take practice. The great thing about this skill is it can also become a habit. The more you do it, the easier it gets, and soon you'll find yourself effortlessly, politely, and firmly declining tasks that don't put your needs and life first without guilt.

For you to say yes to what matters in your life, you're going to have to say no to other things.

Cheers to saying no!

It's not easy saying no, but it is necessary to live life at peace and fulfilled. So, cheers to you saying no more often! Knowing a lot of guilt can come along with this, I want to offer you a guilt-free cocktail.

Sometimes I want a drink, but it's not a good time to drink. I love cocktails made with bubbles (champagne, prosecco, cava, etc.). But in my old age bubbles have gone from the brunch time turnup juice to the bedtime sleep-inducer. If I have more than one mimosa, I get tired. It's really a good thing that my kids are still at a napping age, because after two or three mimosas, I'm ready to lie down on a Saturday afternoon.

Sometimes, though, I know I won't be able to take that nap, and honestly, sometimes I just don't want to be tired. This is where Kombucha Crush comes in. It's low in sugar (so, for me, low in guilt), has enough effervescence to feel fun, and is such a pretty color that I really enjoy sipping it. Just as you are going to drop the guilt related to saying no and trying to do it all, I hope you can sip this worry free.

KOMBUCHA CRUSH

Ingredients

2 to 4 mint leaves, stems removed

½ cup fresh strawberries, stems removed, and sliced (feel free to use frozen strawberries that have been thawed)

1 tablespoon lime juice

6 ounces kombucha (I recommend ginger-flavored kombucha)

½ to 1 ounce vodka (optional)

Instructions

1. In the bottom of a highball glass, muddle the mint leaves, strawberries, and lime juice.
2. Add the kombucha. If you want a splash of alcohol, add the vodka.
3. Fill the rest of the glass with ice.
4. Stir, sip, and delight in what you can now say yes to because you're courageous enough to say no.

4

The 7 Ds of Successful Delegation

DELEGATION HAS BECOME my secret weapon, propelling me toward my goals while leaving room for a little R&R. You see, my goals weren't small; they were big lofty goals.

I knew that to get promoted at work I needed to deliver immense value. For me to savor the time with my family, I had to make sure I was well rested and that my mind and body were healthy. To have some time for me, I needed to ensure the basic needs of our home were met and that I wasn't working long hours on weekends.

All of this meant figuring out a way to ensure the important and urgent things got done without running myself ragged. It meant doing more with less. It meant strategically delegating.

Don't get me wrong: making this shift felt like a lot. I was hesitant and a little scared. But it worked! In just eighteen months, I snagged a promotion to VP (and that was while growing another human inside me). Another eighteen months down the line, and I locked down my first C-suite role.

What was the ace up my sleeve? Delegation. I'm here to tell you it can be yours too.

So what's the hot news? Delegation isn't a superpower. You don't have to be born with the ability to do it; it's a skill you can pick up and get better at along the way. And I'm going to share with you exactly how to delegate so that it amplifies your life.

You're a working mom, a professional powerhouse balancing a demanding career or maybe running your own business, supporting a bustling household, and constantly checking things off a never-ending to-do list. It's a scenario that we navigate every day, often feeling like we must be all things to all people and get everything done.

Delegation is an essential skill that can catapult you toward success by ensuring that important things still get done without you spending time and energy on them. You don't have to take it from me. There are studies and surveys that prove it. There are also studies that show people are often not as effective at delegating as they think they are.

Management expert and business school professor Deborah Grayson Riegel suggests that "delegating, when done well, not only reduces your own workload, it develops your employees, gives you and your team a bigger range of skills and impact, provides emergency back-up (since you're not the only one who knows how to do something), creates inclusive opportunities, empowers people, and retains talent."[1] She also points to several consistent reasons leaders under-delegate:[2]

- They don't know what would actually be helpful to them when it comes to delegating.
- They don't understand how members of their team could benefit from taking on delegated tasks.
- Their bosses or mentors have not shown them how to delegate successfully.
- They believe that delegating may put their own work at risk.

But as much as I love research data, sometimes your gut feeling is the way to go. So to better understand delegating, I want you to come with me on a quick little journey.

Activity

Read through these four questions. Then close your eyes and imagine the possibilities. Finally, write down your answers.

1. What would it be like if you had more time in your workday and less work to take home?
2. What if you didn't have to bring work home and had more time to rest or enjoy being with your family?
3. How would having more time in your day help your career?
4. How would having more time in your day help your home life?

My guess is that having more time in your day would be a wonderful thing. You would not only have time to do other things, but also likely have more energy to spend on those things. Delegation can give that to you.

The art of delegation
is a journey.
Be kind to yourself as you
embark on this path.

The 7 Ds of successful delegation

Alright, Mama, it's time to dive into the nitty-gritty of strategic delegation and craft your plan to reclaim your time, find peace, and even make room for a well-deserved cocktail.

But before we get started, I want to emphasize a few key points. Just like mastering yoga, mastering the art of delegation is a journey. Be kind to yourself as you embark on this path. Remember, if a delegation attempt doesn't go as planned, it's not a failure—it's an opportunity to learn and grow.

Delegation requires effort, but it's an investment that can yield significant returns in terms of time and energy.

Let's focus on defining the 7 Ds of successful delegation. You don't have to internalize all these definitions right now. We'll continue to explore the 7 Ds in greater detail as we take this journey together.

Here's the list:

1 Determine: Assess tasks and decide what to delegate.
2 Define: Specify what success looks like.
3 Decide Who: Select the right people based on skills and capacity.
4 Do the Math: Figure out the time required to teach or explain what you need.
5 Discuss: Clearly communicate the task, expectations, and deadlines.
6 Discourse: Follow up, provide guidance, and evaluate progress.
7 (Happy) Dance: Celebrate your win!

As we embark on this journey together, I'll be with you every step of the way, providing detailed guidance and urging you to take action.

Keep in mind that taking action is crucial to your success. If you're not fully committed to putting in the effort, perhaps this book isn't the right fit for you. However, if you're eager to flourish and take back control of your time, then let's dive in together and make it happen.

Are you ready to commit? (Yes, the answer is yes!)

The benefits of delegation

Here's what delegation can do for you:

- *Amplify your efficiency.* Delegation is like having a team of skilled professionals at your disposal. When you delegate tasks, you're not just passing them off; you're leveraging the expertise of others. This supercharges your efficiency and gets things done faster and oftentimes better.

- *Reduce your stress.* The weight of trying to do it all can be crushing. Delegation acts as a pressure relief valve, releasing the stress and allowing you to breathe.

- *Free up your time.* Time is your most valuable asset. Delegating tasks frees up precious hours in your day. Now you can use that time to be with your kids, to pursue your passions, to take a nap, or simply to enjoy sipping a cocktail on the front porch.

- *Focus on what matters.* Delegation helps you prioritize. You can channel your energy and attention toward tasks that you are best suited to do and that you want to do both at work and in your personal life.

And when you delegate, you are not burdening others, you are supporting them. Here's what others get when you delegate:

You don't have to be born with the ability to delegate; it's a skill you can pick up and get better at along the way.

- *Skills development:* Delegating gives others a chance to flex their skills and expand their know-how. When you toss someone a new responsibility, you're basically saying, "Here's your chance to shine."
- *Increased confidence:* Delegating helps to boost folks' swagger and lets them learn to strut with newfound confidence. When someone realizes they've got what it takes to handle things solo, it's like a superhero discovering their powers.
- *Ownership and accountability:* Delegating instills a sense of ownership and accountability. When people see that you trust them, they invest in delivering.
- *Leadership skills:* Delegating grooms the next generation of leaders. As folks tackle delegated responsibilities, they're not just following orders; they're learning how to call the shots, solve problems, and rally the troops.

- *Time management:* Delegating helps others hone time management skills. It provides an opportunity to learn about balancing priorities and squeezing every ounce of productivity out of their day.

- *Adaptability and resourcefulness:* Delegating gets others to think on their feet and roll with the punches. When folks dive into delegated tasks, they're not just following a recipe; they're MacGyvering their way through unexpected obstacles.

- *Building relationships:* Delegating builds bonds and fosters camaraderie. Delegated tasks give individuals the opportunity to reach out to and meet more people.

- *Career advancement:* Delegating paves the way for career growth. By giving folks a chance to flex their skills and prove their worth, you're not just delegating tasks; you're opening doors to new opportunities and bigger challenges.

- *Empathy:* Delegating is a chance for others to learn what it takes to deliver. It gives them a chance to understand the work you have been doing, and it can build empathy.

Delegation is great—not just for you but for others as well. Take a look at the lists I just shared. We've got four things that delegation can do for you and nine things it can do for others. The biggest thing I want you to take away from this chapter is that, when you delegate, you are providing an opportunity for others.

Now you might be thinking, If delegation is so good, why don't we do it more often? Well, that's what we'll talk about in the next chapter.

But first, cocktails! All that thinking has worked up a powerful thirst.

Cheers to the benefits of delegation!

Sharing is caring, and one of my favorite cocktails to make when people come to my home is a margarita. Now, there are a thousand ways to whip up this classic cocktail, but let me tell you my favorite way. It's simple, really: equal parts tequila, Cointreau, and lime, with just a hint of sugar to balance it all out. So easy, but also so delicious!

Notes

1. Deborah Grayson Riegel, "How to Figure Out If You Have a Problem Delegating—and What to Do about It," *Fast Company*, November 17, 2020.
2. Deborah Grayson Riegel, "8 Ways Leaders Delegate Successfully," *Harvard Business Review*, last updated November 16, 2023.

WHITNEE'S SIMPLE MARGARITA

Ingredients

1½ ounces white tequila

1½ ounces Cointreau (seriously, this is the secret sauce; don't you dare reach for another brand of triple sec... step away from the bottom-shelf orange liqueur)

1½ ounces lime juice

1 teaspoon white sugar, to taste

Instructions

1. Put everything in a cocktail shaker.
2. Fill the shaker with ice cubes.
3. Shake, shake, shake, Senora, until the shaker is super cold to the touch, about 15 to 20 seconds.
4. Pour the drink into a glass filled with ice.
5. Take a sip and say cheers to the power of delegation.

5

Busting the Myths That Keep Us from Delegating

READY TO get to the 7 Ds? I'm ready to share them with you, but first we need to break through any ideas that might keep you from delegating. Many of us struggle to delegate and once we start, we can easily backslide into our old ways. I know I did. I also know that over time I've gotten better and better at it, and you can too. Having the right mindset has helped me be persistent and consistent.

I first realized the need to delegate when I got promoted at work from an analyst to a manager. When I was an analyst, I had to do it all myself. I was an independent contributor, and me doing the work is what got the work done. Then I got promoted. Suddenly, I was responsible for a team of people. I found myself working harder and longer than ever before. Everything that was given to our team, I played some part in completing.

I remember, one time, my director asked for an analysis on the latest in airport lobby technology (I worked for an airline). I let my team know that this report needed to be completed by the end of the week and then I started working on it. On Wednesday, the report was coming along pretty well, but I needed to include a few more statistics. I reached out to one of my direct reports, let's call him Sean, to ask for the information (look at me delegating!). To my surprise, he sent it to me right away. I thought, Man, this guy is good. I left for the day and planned to wrap everything up Thursday.

Thursday came, and as I opened my inbox, you will not believe what I saw. A draft of the same report I had been working on, from Sean. Can you imagine? We had both spent the week doing the same work. And here's the kicker: his report was actually better than mine! It had all the right information and was so pretty. His charts, graphs, and tables were perfectly aligned, and the colors he chose popped but were not gaudy. I was impressed, frustrated, and scared. Impressed, because, man, it was a great report. Frustrated because of the duplicate work—both of us doing the same report was a waste of time. Scared, because he did it better than me, and I was worried that could mean he was coming for my job or that my director would think I was a bad manager.

I was paralyzed by these emotions and fear. I didn't know what to do. I thought if I turned in his report, my director might think I was being lazy and off-loading my work onto the team. Or he might question why he had even hired me in the first place. I thought, even though Sean's report was better than mine, maybe I should still turn mine in. At the end of the day, Sean's was better so that was what I turned in.

After reviewing the report, my director sent me an email saying something to the effect of "Thanks for the report; this is exactly what I needed. Sean did a great job. Awesome to see you developing the team."

"Awesome to see you developing the team"???? I was dumbfounded; none of my fears came true. I was not less valuable because someone else had done the work (and done it better than me). My mind was blown.

Having spoken with and coached other women, I know my story isn't the only one like this. I also know being worried about how you'll be seen isn't the only reason we don't delegate.

I've found that there are four key reasons we shy away from delegation.

1 You've been burned in the past by delegating.
2 No one can do it like you can.
3 It takes too much time.
4 You'll be less valuable.

While these "reasons" may feel very real to you, I've come to learn that they aren't reasons and instead are myths. Your belief in them is holding you back from advancing your career and living a life you love.

So let's bust these myths, replace them with facts, and then learn how to effectively apply the art of strategic delegation to get more peace and live fulfilled.

Delegation—at home, at work, and everywhere else—helps us be more impactful in the areas of our life that move the needle and fill our hearts.

Myth 1: You've been burned in the past by delegating

Mama, just because something fails once doesn't mean it will never work. Successfully delegating isn't always easy but it is doable. What's even better is that delegating is a skill. Which means, unlike a talent that you are simply born with, you can learn to develop your ability to delegate. Later in this book we'll go through exactly what you should and should not delegate as well as the exact steps you can take to ensure a successful outcome every time.

There is a right and wrong way to delegate. I am going to teach you the right way, so you never get burned again.

Myth 2: No one can do it like you can

Can't nobody do it like you. Well, it's likely true. No one can do it like you can. But that does not mean you should not delegate it. Just because someone can't do it exactly like you does not mean they can't give you a successful outcome. There are two key factors that tend to come into play when "no one can do it like me" is given as the reason to not delegate.

1. In reality, it's not that they can't do it like you; it's that you have not fully defined a successful outcome.
2. Either you were not able to delegate to someone with the skills to deliver or you didn't take the time to teach them (more on this later).

Let me illustrate the point with a personal story.

In my household, I do the cooking. I plan the meals, I shop for the food, and I prepare what we eat. My husband is fully capable of doing these things. I met the man when he was in his late thirties, and he was feeding himself, all by himself. Also, he's from Louisiana; he knows the flavor. Still, I enjoy cooking, and my family seems to enjoy my food. So I cook and he cleans.

Well, one day I was running late from work. So I texted him to ask if he could make dinner. There was red pasta sauce in the fridge, so I asked him to make spaghetti. He texted back that he could, and I focused on getting home. I walked in just in time for us to sit down to dinner. To my horror, what did I see: noodles with sauce on top and no vegetables. Meanwhile, he had this proud look on his face like "mission accomplished."

I was so frustrated.

It was because my husband didn't make the spaghetti like I make spaghetti, which is the noodles simmered in the sauce. He also didn't make dinner like I make dinner, with veggies on the plate. I was about to say something to my husband when I saw my son gobbling up his noodles. It was the sign I needed to take a beat and breathe. In that breath I realized there is more than one way to make spaghetti. I also realized that I only asked him to use the red sauce in the fridge to make dinner. I wasn't specific on how to apply it. I didn't tell him to include veggies. I had failed to articulate the successful outcomes. Still, we had a hot nutritious meal (we use protein pasta) to eat.

He didn't do it like I did, but it got done, and I got what I really wanted: a hot dinner for my family.

Remember, as you are telling yourself, "No one can do it like me," there is more than one way to make spaghetti. And don't forget to share the whole recipe.

Myth 3: It takes too much time

I often hear: "It takes too much time to delegate." And, you know, sometimes it does and sometimes it doesn't. The one thing that is always true is, it does take time to delegate. You have to prepare to effectively delegate. You may need to teach someone how to do the task. You'll need to check in from time to time on the progress. Delegation takes time. But how much time is too much time? This is where the delegation equation comes in. Later in this book, I'll teach the back-of-the-envelope equation you can do to see whether delegating is the right investment of your precious time.

Myth 4: You'll be less valuable

This is the one that breaks my heart. Maybe it's because of how much I see my younger self in this "reason" not to delegate, or maybe it's because, at the end of the day, I know that your self-worth is not about what you do but about what you don't do.

You see, when we are trying to do all the things, it spreads us thin and stops us from being able to deliver the important things with quality. Remember how I spent a week working on a report that my direct report could have easily handled? Well you know what that meant? It meant I didn't get to put the time and effort I would have into a presentation I was preparing for one of our company's vice presidents. My value to the company would have shown up a lot stronger and been more impactful if I had spent the time I put into that report on the presentation instead.

To be sure, this doesn't just show up at work. It shows up at home. There was a time when I thought that as a good mom,

I should be doing all the things. Even though I could afford a house cleaner, I should be cleaning the house. But then I had to step back and think: Wow, with the two to three hours it takes to do a full clean of the house each week, could I be doing something more valuable? And the answer was yes. There were way more valuable things I could do with that time, such as the following:

1. Play with my son.
2. Read up on topics that will help me at work.
3. Take a nap so I'm less cranky.
4. Crotchet.
5. Take a walk with my family.

By *not* being the one to clean my house, I could actually be a better mom and add more value to my family.

Delegation—at home, at work, and everywhere else—helps us be more impactful in the areas of our life that move the needle and fill our hearts.

Cheers to moving past the myths and into a new reality!

We need to embrace a reality where we own our part in successful delegation and release the ideas that hold us back from delegating, and we need to do this in a way that lets us focus on what matters most. Still, it's not easy to make that shift. In order to do this, from time to time we may need to give ourselves a little tough love, love that is strong like a stiff drink. One that gets straight to the point like a mint julep.

The second time I had a mint julep, I nearly fell off my barstool. You see, the first time I had one, it wasn't really a mint julep. I was at a dive bar in Lower Manhattan, and it was the Kentucky Derby weekend. (Yep, we celebrate it all the way up in NYC too.) The bar had five-dollar special juleps, and I thought when you're in a fancy hat, day drinking at a dive bar pretending to be at the derby you might as well have that signature cocktail. What was served that day may have been someone's signature drink, but it wasn't the derby's. Looking back, I'm pretty sure the bar was serving up Sprite with bourbon and a mint leaf on the top—not bad, but also not a real julep.

Flash forward to a brunch later that summer at a friend-of-a-friend's apartment. She was from Kentucky and offered us juleps. She actually had those special glasses you see people on TV drinking them in. So I thought, I'll give it a go. I had my first sip. I gasped. It was sooo delicious... and strong. It tasted like tough love in a glass to me. I absolutely loved it, and to this day, on a hot evening, it's one of my favorite porch-sippers to end the day with.

MINT JULEP

Ingredients

8 to 10 fresh mint leaves

2 ounces bourbon

1 teaspoon sugar, to taste

Sprig of fresh mint, for garnish

Instructions

1. In a cocktail shaker, muddle the mint leaves gently to release their oils.
2. Add the bourbon and the sugar to the shaker. Add ice cubes and shake until the shaker feels cold, about 15 to 20 seconds.
3. Fill a rocks glass with crushed ice and pour the cocktail into the glass.
4. Garnish with a sprig of fresh mint.
5. Serve immediately and enjoy your refreshing Mint Julep!

Note: Adjust the amount of sugar to suit your taste. You can also dissolve the sugar in a little water before adding it to the glass if you prefer.

6

Determine: Assess Tasks and Decide What to Delegate

ALRIGHT, WE CAN all agree that delegation is good for us and others. We know that some of the "reasons" we've been telling ourselves we can't delegate are really myths. I've also shared that some tasks are ripe for delegation, and some should stay in our own capable hands. So let's roll up our sleeves and dive into the juicy details of what needs to be done and what we can confidently pass on to someone else.

First things first, to effectively delegate you have to know what's important to you. You gotta be clear on where you want to spend your time and where you don't. You have to know what areas are going to move the needle for your career, home, and heart.

Activity

Let's take a moment to ensure you have the clarity you need to effectively delegate. Earlier, I mentioned the nine areas of life. Take a moment to write down what you want out of each area over the next 365 days. This list will help guide you in two ways: you'll be clear on what things you are doing today that are not moving the needle for you, and you'll have a reference sheet for where to spend your time as you free it up.

1. Career/work
2. Relationship with kids
3. Health
4. Relationship with partner, self, or if you're single and ready to mingle... dating
5. Finances
6. Personal growth
7. Fun and adventure
8. Physical environment
9. Community and giving back

Now that you are clear on what you want, let's get more specific on what and what not to delegate.

What to delegate

1. *Routine and repetitive tasks:* Delegating these tasks is normally straightforward, and once someone else learns how to do it, they can keep doing it. Often, completing routine and repetitive tasks is not the best use of your time. By assigning these to someone else, you free up your own time to focus on more strategic and high-impact activities that can help you shine or move the needle on your heart.

2. *Tasks outside your expertise:* If you aren't a pro at something and someone else is, delegate that task—this is a clear opportunity to save time and will likely result in a better outcome. There is a caveat here: if you want to build expertise in that area, then don't delegate it. But if, for example, like me, you are not that great at making reports pretty and you don't care to become an expert in it, then let someone else use their skills here.

3. *Time-consuming activities:* If something takes you a long time to do and neither do you enjoy it nor does it help you shine, then delegating can free you up to do the things that will allow you to flourish.

4. *Tasks with clear instructions:* Whatever the task, if it's not moving your needle and it has clear instructions, it's a winner for delegating.

5. *Tasks that promote skills development:* If there is something on your plate, even if you are great at it, but it helps someone else develop a skill, it's a great thing to delegate. By assigning challenging and growth-oriented tasks, you enable your team (and family) members to expand their capabilities, gain new experiences, and enhance their skill sets. Moreover, delegating such tasks demonstrates

your trust in their abilities and fosters a culture of continuous learning and development.

6 *Tasks where others have expertise:* Delegating tasks to individuals with expertise in a particular area allows you to leverage their specialized knowledge and skills effectively. Rather than attempting to tackle complex or specialized tasks yourself, even if you can, entrusting them to someone with the necessary expertise ensures that they are completed proficiently and with optimal results.

Now that you have the list of what to delegate, let's talk about what not to delegate.

What not to delegate

1 *Core work responsibilities:* Your core work responsibilities are, well, your bread and butter. These are the tasks that define your role and contribute directly to your success. Delegating them to someone else can undermine your credibility and authority, not to mention jeopardize the quality of your work. So unless you want to risk your reputation, it's best to keep these tasks on your plate. If you're unsure what is core to your role, check in with your manager.

2 *Strategic decision-making:* Strategic decision-making is the essence of leadership. It involves analyzing complex information, weighing various options, and charting the course for your team or organization. Delegating such critical decisions can dilute your influence and lead to misalignment or confusion. When it comes to strategic matters, the buck stops with you.

Delegating tasks to individuals
with expertise in a particular area
allows you to leverage
their specialized knowledge
and skills effectively.

3 *Tasks that require your unique skills:* You've got skills, talents, and expertise that set you apart from the rest. These are the tasks that only you can do justice to, thanks to your unique perspective and capabilities. Delegating them would be like asking Pablo Picasso to let someone else paint his masterpiece—it just doesn't make sense. So hold on to these tasks and let your brilliance shine.

4 *Tasks that require immediate attention:* Some tasks simply can't wait. They require swift action and decisive leadership to prevent issues from escalating or opportunities from slipping away. Delegating such time-sensitive tasks can lead to delays, missed deadlines, or even crises. When the clock is ticking, it's best to roll up your sleeves and tackle the task head-on.

5 *Tasks you don't have time to teach:* Delegating isn't just about off-loading tasks; it's also about empowering others through guidance and mentorship. If you don't have the time or bandwidth to properly train someone on a task, delegating it could set them up for failure—and you for frustration. It's better to hold on to the task until you can provide the necessary support.

6 *Tasks where it will take you longer to teach than to do them (overtime):* Time is money, as they say. If teaching someone to do a task will eat up more time than simply doing it yourself, it's probably not worth delegating. While investing in skills development is crucial, there are times when efficiency trumps everything else. So before you hand off a task, weigh the time investment against the potential payoff and choose wisely. I'll show you how to use the delegation equation for this in chapter 9.

7 *Tasks that move your heartstrings:* If there are things you love to do, then do them. One thing I absolutely adore is going to the grocery store. I love to walk up and down the aisles, look at the products, and think about new ways I could use them. So while I do delegate my grocery shopping on occasion, I also take the time to handle this task on my own because it fills me.

Another way to think about tasks that move your heartstrings is to go with your gut. Trust what feels right. One day, when my oldest was about seven months old, I took him on a business trip with me. I had a conference to attend and a trusted friend in the same city to watch him. Now, traveling with a baby means moving around with a lot of stuff. I had my suitcase, a stroller, a diaper bag, a car seat, and, of course, the baby. As I was boarding, no, struggling to board the plane, some friendly folks offered to help.

I had made it to my seat, but with the baby strapped to my chest, I couldn't quite manage to get my carry-on suitcase into the overhead bin. A very friendly man from across the aisle called out, "Would you like some help?"

"Yes, thank you so much!" I said.

But as I went to hand him the carry-on, he reached out and said, "I'll take the baby."

No, sir, you will not.

I was overwhelmed in the moment and needed help, and I needed to delegate something, but it was clear that delegating the baby was not the answer.

"Thank you, but it would be most helpful if you could just put this carry-on in the bin," I replied.

Holding the baby tugged at my heartstrings, and my gut screamed that handing over my child was not the right move.

So I found another way to get the support I needed by asking him to help with the luggage.

As you think through what you do and don't want to delegate, remember to hold on to your babies.

Activity

You've taken the time to write down what's important to you in each area of life. But to truly embody that person and attain those goals, you need to clear your plate. Now it's time to put the delegation dos and don'ts list into action.

Take a moment to jot down everything you'd like to delegate. This will now be known as your not-for-me-to-do list.

Don't stress if you're unsure who will handle these tasks.

Don't worry if you're unsure about the process or logistics.

Don't fret if you think it might take too much time to delegate.

Now take a good look at your list and pinpoint the one task that would make the biggest splash if you were to delegate it. We're going to tackle that one first. I know, it's tempting to want to delegate everything on your list right this minute but remember: slow and steady wins the delegation race. We'll focus on delegating that high-impact task first, step by step. Then once that's taken care of, you can circle back and tackle the next item on your list, and so on. Before you know it, your list will be cleared, and you'll be on your way to flourishing.

Feeling stuck on where to start with delegation? Ask yourself these guiding questions:

1 What task are you currently working on that doesn't allow you to shine or be your best?

Delegating isn't just about off-loading tasks; it's also about empowering others through guidance and mentorship.

2 What activity brings up feelings of sadness, anger, or annoyance whenever you have to do it?

3 What's on your to-do list that you simply dread tackling?

These questions can help pinpoint tasks that are ripe for delegation. Examples include slide design, data analysis, people management, household chores like laundry or cleaning, meal preparation, or drop-offs and pickups. Now that you've got your task in mind, jot it down.

What are you committed to delegating this week? Let's make it happen!

Cheers to a good list!

I love a good list. Seriously, I adore one, and if you haven't gotten the vibe yet, I make them for almost everything. For me, writing things down both makes them real and highlights the misleading thoughts in my head. Like when I tell myself I have one thousand things to do, but in reality, I have twenty-two. A great list can indeed be as satisfying as a great cocktail. One of my absolute favorite drinks is called a Paper Plane. I've chosen this one because, like a good list, it's both refreshing and complex.

One day, I was planning a happy hour for some of my colleagues (we all worked for an airline), and I started googling aviation-themed drinks. A drink called Aviation came up repeatedly. It's made with gin, and I do not like gin. (Please note, there are zero gin cocktails in this book.) I thought about just substituting it with vodka but gave the old Google one last go and found this drink. I am a fan of all the ingredients, so I thought it was worth giving a try. I was super-impressed with how easy it was to make and yet how complex it tasted. This is a go-to for me at home or when I'm out. If you don't see it on the menu, just ask for all four ingredients in equal parts, shaken, and poured in a coupe or martini glass!

PAPER PLANE

Ingredients

¾ ounce bourbon

¾ ounce Aperol

¾ ounce Amaro Nonino

¾ ounce fresh lemon juice

Orange peel, for garnish

Instructions

1. Fill a cocktail shaker with ice cubes.
2. Add the bourbon, Aperol, Amaro Nonino, and fresh lemon juice to the shaker.
3. Shake well until the mixture is chilled, about 15 to 20 seconds.
4. Strain the mixture into a chilled coupe glass.
5. Garnish with an orange peel.
6. Serve and enjoy your refreshing Paper Plane while you think about your delegation list.

7

Define: Specify What Success Looks Like

CHANGE IS HARD for all of us. It's most difficult to deal with when it's unexpected. At work, we expect people to come to us for support. We expect our leaders to delegate tasks to us, we anticipate that a colleague might need help here and there, but at home, this expectation may not be there.

At home, our partners, children, and anyone else we live with may not expect that we would delegate to them. The thought of being delegated to may have never even crossed their minds. Just because they aren't expecting it, it doesn't mean it can't happen. Just because they aren't anticipating it, it doesn't mean it's wrong. Just because they would rather not take on additional responsibilities, it doesn't mean you don't deserve to delegate. It just means you need to take an extra step in preparing your household for your newfound superpower of delegation.

There are three ingredients you can add to your definition of success to make things go more smoothly at home: pre-communication, grace, and persistence. I'll dive into those three secret ingredients and how you can get them to work, but first, let's just re-up the importance of delegating and reaffirm that you deserve this.

Let's start with why

Your value as a mother and a partner is not about how many clothes you fold, toilets you clean, or meals you cook. What you do for others does not determine your worth. And if your family is telling you the story that your doing everything for everyone in your house is what they need from you, I challenge that.

A lot of times, as women, we tend to want to help and support our family. Whether I'm heating up leftover pancakes or making my oldest son's favorite Texa-Cajun chicken, I get deep satisfaction from preparing and serving a meal. When I look around the living room and the floor is toy-free, I feel satisfied. Still, the entirety of parenting and housekeeping is not solely my cross to bear. Our family is a community. We are all members of the community and have a part to play. More often than not, I have to remind myself of a few things:

- The role I've been conditioned into, of default parent and housekeeper, is not the role that helps me flourish.
- When I am worn out and cranky from being stretched too thin, I am not showing up as the best wife or mom.
- Giving my kids the opportunity to take on more around the house is preparing them to be better humans and independent adults.
- Sharing the workload with my husband, who is a fully competent and capable human, is healthy; taking everything on myself is not.

After my son was born, I had this idea of myself that I would be the woman to "have and do it all." Hot meals, sparkling windows, waxed floors, adorably dressed children, and on, and on, and on. Some of those things, I came to realize, were not really my priority (please note the ongoing case of mismatched socks on my son's feet). Other things I realized I wanted but just couldn't keep up with while also growing my career.

I started to delegate those tasks or eliminate them completely from my life and schedule. But as new things came up for our family, I would often find myself being the one to take them on. We needed to call the super to get the kitchen sink fixed. I did it. There was an "event" at the day care and they needed snacks. I got them. A friend was coming to visit, and we needed a new air mattress and sheets. I researched, shopped for, ordered, and set them up. I did it. Why? Because the role I had assumed for myself was the person who just did it.

And my husband was happy to let me do it all.

Over time, it became the expectation that I would do all these things. Why? Because I had always done them. And I started to wonder why. I was doing them partly because I was on autopilot and partly because I thought it was what

I needed to start
delegating at home so
I could be the best
me possible: joyful,
present, and energized.

I should do to be a good mom and wife. Well, we've talked about should. I realized I was should-ing on myself.

Did it make me a better wife because I washed the windows? Was I a great mom because I enrolled and took my son to Mommy and Me classes every weekend? NO! In fact, trying to do those things made me a worse wife and mom. It made me irritable and resentful. I was tired and angry and sad. Not exactly the kind of woman my husband wanted to be around and not the kind of mom who is the most nurturing and calm with her baby. I realized I needed to start delegating at home. Why? So I could be the best me possible: joyful, present, and energized, which would allow me to be the best mom and wife possible.

If you've been playing the role of default parent and housekeeper, and it brings you down, that is your why. Hold on to that and work through this with your family. Your family will expect you to continue playing the role you always have; the good news is that those expectations can change. The great news is that if this role isn't working for you, it's actually not working for them either (you are not being the best mom or wife when you are overwhelmed and exhausted). So when the change comes and you start delegating more, everyone will benefit.

TO SUCCESSFULLY delegate you have to be able to clearly define what success looks like. If you don't define success up front and instead leave it to interpretation, you'll likely not get what you were looking for.

For example, say I ask someone to make the bed for me. Now there are over a hundred different ways to make a bed. Here are two ways, and I need you tell me which was successful:

Person A picks the comforter up off the floor, throws it on the bed, straightens it so it's mostly flat, and throws all the pillows against the headboard.

Person B securely fastens the fitted sheet. Makes hospital corners with the top sheet. Then they bounce a quarter off the top sheet to be sure it's secure. Smooths the comforter across the bed. Places the pillows along the headboard and pillow-chops them so they look neat.

Person A may have grown up in a home where making the bed was an afterthought. Person B may have grown up with military parents. Success looks very different for them because of their different past experiences.

There you have a bit of backstory and two very different ways to make a bed. Which one was successful?

Wait for it... you don't know. Why? Because success was never defined.

Now had I said, "Hey, we are in a rush and need to get out of the house, but the cleaner is coming, and I need the beds made with the covers and pillows off the floor, so she can vacuum," Person A did the best job. Person B spent too much time given our urgency.

If I said, "My aunt is coming to town, and she is particular about her sleeping space. I need a tightly made bed to help reduce any potential drama," then Person A clearly failed, and Person B succeeded.

Without your defining success, it's impossible to know what outcome you'll get. Defining success is about painting the picture of the outcome you'd like and defining any required key performance indicators (KPIs).

But defining success can be challenging, because sometimes you only know it's right when you see it. One effective way to clarify what success looks like is through visualization. If you're struggling to define success, try literally drawing a picture. In this picture, identify the key elements that signify completion and success for you.

Success should be defined clearly and quantitatively, outlining specific outcomes and criteria. For example, when I ask someone to prepare a presentation, I include the following details:

- the completion date (e.g., May 7 or two weeks before the quarterly board meeting)
- specific outcomes (e.g., a report on fourth-quarter [Q4] numbers with monthly, weekly, and daily breakdowns by customer type)

Another example is delegating management of a project. I might say: "I want you to be responsible for the team delivering this spreadsheet. The spreadsheet and report need to be completed by the thirtieth of the month, including breakdowns from each account with both historical and future-looking data. Additionally, provide some analysis of what these numbers mean and put the information into a PowerPoint presentation. We should review this together two weeks before the due date to make any necessary revisions."

By being clear and detailed in defining success, you ensure that everyone involved understands the expectations and can work toward the desired outcomes efficiently.

Activity

Now take a task you want to delegate and write down what success looks like. Is it hospital corners and a top sheet so tight you can bounce a quarter off it? Is it a typo-free memo that has good grammar? Is it a report completed by X date with supporting charts?

The more clearly you can create the picture of success and the more specific you can measure the outcomes you want, the better the person you are delegating to will be able to deliver.

Write out what a successful outcome for your delegated task looks like. Be as descriptive as you can and include as many KPIs as possible.

8

Decide Who: Select the Right People Based on Skills and Capacity

WHILE THE CORE SKILLS required to delegate at work and at home are the same, the expectations in each place can be different. At work there is an expectation of shared responsibilities. Deciding whom to delegate to is often a matter of simply identifying the right member of your team.

At home, that expectation may not exist; so, first things first, we need to create that expectation.

Initiating a no-holds-barred chat with your crew about the dire need for delegation is step one in this household revolution. Lay it all out on the table: the chaos, the craziness, and how it's impacting you. Remind your family that you are part of a community, and you must work together to deliver.

Sell them on the idea that delegation isn't just about lightening your load—it's about creating more quality fam time and making sure everyone pulls their weight. Open up the floor to hear their concerns.

Make sure it's clear that everyone's time is equally valuable and it's not about counting who does what, for how many hours each week, but instead making sure that everyone is contributing based on their abilities.

When you talk through this new family future, share the 7 Ds with them. Let each family member know that their contributions will match their abilities, you'll take the time to train them if it's needed, and there will be rewards and recognition (happy dances) for the work they do.

Grace

Embarking on the delegation journey is like setting out on a wild adventure through uncharted territory. It's thrilling, it's daunting, and it's bound to have a few bumps along the way. So strap in and get ready for the ride of your life. But amidst the chaos and uncertainty, one thing is certain: grace is your trusty companion.

First and foremost, extend that grace to yourself. You're stepping into uncharted waters and navigating unexplored terrain, and that's no small feat. Cut yourself some slack, Mama. Rome wasn't built in a day, and neither is a well-delegated household. Embrace the learning curve, celebrate the victories, and learn from the setbacks. You're doing the best you can, and that's more than enough.

Now let's talk about extending that grace to your family. They're your partners in this delegation dance, your comrades in arms. But they're also human, with their own quirks, limitations, and learning curves. So be patient. Give 'em space to adjust, room to grow, and time to find their footing. Remember, teamwork makes the dream work, and that means supporting each other through the ups and downs.

And finally, don't forget to sprinkle a little grace over the entire delegation process. It's messy, it's unpredictable, but it's also incredibly rewarding. Embrace the journey, the twists and turns, the highs and lows. Trust that every stumble is a step forward; every setback, a lesson learned. So take a deep breath and hold on to that grace, and let's dive headfirst into the wild and wonderful world of delegation.

Persistence

Alright, Mama, let's talk about the inevitable pushback you're bound to encounter on your delegation journey. Brace yourself, because it's coming, and it's coming from the people closest to you: your family. They mean well, but change is hard, and they might resist at first.

Get ready to hear some familiar refrains.

First up: "You do this so much better than me." Ah, the classic comparison trap. Your family members may feel intimidated by your expertise, fearing they won't measure up. Remind them that everyone starts somewhere, and practice makes progress. Encourage them to give it a try and assure them that mistakes are part of the learning process.

Next: "I'll never learn to do this." Cue the defeatist attitude. It's natural for your loved ones to feel overwhelmed by new tasks, especially if they've never done them before. Be patient and offer gentle guidance. Break the task down into manageable steps, and celebrate every small victory along the way.

Cut yourself some slack, Mama.
Embrace the learning curve,
celebrate the victories,
and learn from the setbacks.

Then there's the timeless excuse: "It takes too long." Ah, the age-old plea for efficiency. Your family members may balk at the idea of adding new responsibilities to their plates, fearing they will eat up precious time. Remind them that delegation isn't just about lightening your load; it's about empowering them to take ownership and contribute to the household.

And let's not forget: "I have more important things to do." Ah, the prioritization predicament. Your family members may struggle to see the value in the tasks you're delegating, viewing them as less important than their own to-do list. Help them understand the bigger picture and how their contributions fit into the overall goal of creating a balanced and harmonious household.

Last but not least: "You didn't remind me to do it." Ah, the blame game. Your family members may try to shift responsibility onto you, claiming they forgot because you didn't remind them. Encourage accountability by establishing clear expectations and communication channels. Remind them that delegation is a team effort, and everyone plays a part in its success.

So, there you have it, Mama. When the pushback comes knocking, stand your ground but do so with empathy and understanding. Address each concern with patience and positivity, and before you know it, your family will be on board with the delegation game plan.

What resources can you access to help you gain the support required?

In this instance, resources refer to both money and people. Whether you are looking to delegate something at work or at home, you need to consider what funding and which people are available. Who on your team or in your sphere has the ability to do this?

At work or at home, when you look around at the team and people you have access to, how capable are they of the task? It's important to define whether the person is an expert, a novice, or someone in-between. Knowing this will help you to figure out how much time it may take to explain the task. And if you'll need to teach them, how much time that might take. For example, if you want help running a report and have identified an analyst who runs reports all the time, you can consider them an expert. If you want your six-year-old to start helping with the laundry, they would likely be considered a novice.

It may seem like delegating to kids is more trouble than it's worth. You might think it's easier to just do it yourself. However, consider how many times these tasks will be done over the years they live with you. Starting them young with household responsibilities is a worthwhile investment.

In our home, we assign age-appropriate tasks to our kids, who have been helping out since they were two and four. For example, they assist with laundry. A simple task for them is separating clothes by colors. When you break down tasks into smaller steps, it becomes easier to delegate. For laundry, they can sort clothes into piles of colors, whites, and darks, and even load the washing machine or unload the dryer.

Another task they handle is table cleanup. We provide tools suited for their small hands, such as handheld vacuums and dustpans. After meals, they clean the floor. Do I sometimes have to clean up after them? Yes, but it's a fantastic way to get them started and teach responsibility.

Think about:
- budget (household or work),
- team (let's say your family and friends are your number one team),
- contractors (whether it's a business process operator, local handyperson, or consultant, is there someone you can pay to do this?).

Thinking about the person you've identified, you should ask yourself these questions:
- What is their current expertise?
- What is their ability to learn?
- What is their desire to be showcased in this way?

Once you've decided whom you'll delegate to, the next step is to start to think about how much time you'll need to invest in them. If they're an expert, it shouldn't take too long. Given you just wrote down what success looks like, a short phone call or email may suffice. If they're a novice, you will need to set aside some time to teach them. Think about how long that might take. We'll use this information in the next chapter, in a delegation equation, and decide if it's worth the time investment to delegate.

Activity

Write down:
- Who will do the task that you need doing?
- Are they an expert, novice, or in-between?
- How long will it take to share a successful outcome with them?
- How long will it take to teach them (if required)?

Don't forget to sprinkle a little grace over the entire delegation process.

As I mentioned, I've been delegating for a while now, but it didn't always come naturally to me. I remember a time when I was delegating a project to a team member I got along with really well. We had about twenty minutes set aside to discuss the project, but she started telling me about her weekend, and we ended up chatting the entire time. When I checked the clock, I realized we only had a few minutes left, so I quickly tried to cover everything: "I need you to do this report, get it to me by this date, and here's what it involves." You can guess she left the meeting a bit confused and not fully prepared to deliver the work I needed.

Since then, I've found that writing a script in advance helps me have the right discussion with my team. So I'm sharing the script I use with you.

At the end of the book (in the section Extra, Extra), I've provided additional templates and examples for delegating at work, at home, and with your kids. Refer to this guide any time you want a helping hand.

Feel free to adjust any details to better fit your voice and context!

Start with an introduction

I hope you're doing well. We are here today to talk because I need to delegate an important task to you and want to provide all the necessary details to ensure it's completed successfully.

Provide a task description

The task I need you to work on is [briefly describe the task or project]. Specifically, you will be responsible for [provide a detailed description of what the task entails].

Share expectations

To ensure the task is completed to the required standard, here are the key expectations.

1. Objective: The primary objective of this task is [explain the main goal or purpose].

2. Deliverables: The deliverables for this task include [list the specific outcomes, documents, or results that need to be produced].

3. Quality standards: The quality standards to be maintained are [mention any specific quality criteria or standards that need to be met].

Set deadlines

The deadlines for this task are as follows.

1. Initial draft/progress report: [Due date for the initial draft or progress report]

2. Review meetings: [Dates of review meetings to discuss the progress and any necessary adjustments, as required]

3. Final submission: [Due date for the final deliverable]

Offer resources

You can access the following resources to help you complete the task.

1. [Resource 1: e.g., documents, templates, software tools]
2. [Resource 2]
3. [Resource 3]

Show support

If you have any questions or need further assistance, please don't hesitate to reach out. I'm here to support you and ensure you have everything you need to succeed.

Set time for follow-up

We will have a follow-up meeting on [date] to review the progress and address any challenges you might be facing. Please ensure you are ready to discuss your progress by then.

Reassure they are capable (closing)

Thank you for taking on this task. I'm confident in your ability to complete it successfully. Let's touch base [date, tomorrow, next week, etc.] to ensure everything is on track.

9

Do the Math: Figure Out the Time Required to Teach What You Need

WHEN I WORKED in IT, I created and ran a report every month. It had details on our spending; the resource hours used; the Red, Amber, Green status of various projects; and any pertinent project details. Given projects were managed across multiple systems and across various teams, it took several hours to compile and disseminate the report.

When I first created it, I was very proud of the report, and it gave me some great visibility with the senior leaders in my company whom it was designed for. When I first started doing the report, it was a great use of my time and skills. It required critical thinking skills to understand what needed to go into the report, analytic skills to process the report, relationship-building skills to ensure I was getting the latest and greatest on project updates, executive-level presence to sit and review with any execs who wanted a deeper dive into the report, and more.

As time went on and I refined the process of how the report was made, while the report still gave me good exposure, it started to feel a bit boring, and by that time I had other means of exposure to our senior leaders. I knew it was time to delegate my report, but I thought, Man, it's going to take me sooo long to teach someone how to do this and a lot of time to review their work before sending it out. It's better if I keep doing it.

Then I used the delegation equation, and you know what? I found out I was wrong.

It took me 4 hours to complete the report each month. I reasoned that I could teach someone how to do it in about 3 hours and that it would take me about 1.5 hours to review and make corrections each month. When I did the math, I saw

- (T)ime it takes to complete the task: 4 hours
- (N)umber of times you'll do the task in the next three to twelve months: 12
- (R)equired time to teach the task: 3 hours
- (O)utcomes review: 18 hours (1.5 hours × 12 times)

What I got was I was spending this much time on that report each year: 4 hours × 12 = 48 hours.

And I saw that it would take me a total of 21 hours to teach and review the report.

So, 48 hours > 21 hours.

I could actually save over 25 hours each year if I delegated. Boy, was I wrong about it taking too long.

I immediately made a plan to delegate the report, and you know what? It worked out great. The person I delegated to was excited to take on the high-visibility work and learn new skill sets, and I was thrilled to be done creating it each month and have over 25 hours back in my workdays.

Successfully delegating takes an investment of your time and energy

Alright, let's talk about time and energy, two peas in a pod but definitely not twins. Picture this: you've got a pile of laundry lying around the house (or maybe that's just me). Sure, you've got a spare ten minutes to tackle it, but do you have the energy? Probably not. Time may be there, but energy? Well, that's a whole different ball game.

Unlike time, which sticks to its twenty-four-hour routine, energy is a wild card. It can soar one moment and nose-dive the next, depending on how much sleep you got, what you ate for breakfast, and whether the kids decided to have a dance party at 6:00 a.m. on a Saturday. So while time stays put, energy does its own unpredictable dance.

Now here's where things get interesting. Delegation isn't just about freeing up time, it's about mastering the art of energy management. By off-loading those energy-draining tasks—such as folding laundry or manipulating PowerPoint slides—we're not just saving time, we're reclaiming our mojo.

Think of it as a power move. Instead of spreading yourself thin trying to do it all, delegation lets you channel your energy into the things that light you up. It lets you have more

Delegation isn't just about
freeing up time,
it's about mastering the art
of energy management.

impact by freeing you up to focus on your priorities while the other work still gets done.

You have only twenty-four hours in a day, and your energy depletes throughout the day and eventually can burn out (see what I did there). So how do you get more out of finite time and the precious but limited resource of energy? You delegate.

Another way to think of it is to visualize a math question where leveraging delegation allows you to have more impact.

Time + Energy < (Time + Energy) Delegation

Time refers to the fixed and finite resource we all have, measured in hours, days, weeks, and so on.

Energy represents your mental, physical, and emotional vitality—the fuel that powers your actions and productivity.

You can't increase your time, so your energy will ultimately deplete; therefore, to get more, you have to delegate. Delegating allows you to be greater.

We want to be sure you are getting a return on the investment and that's where the delegation equation comes in. Now don't get nervous; this isn't super complicated—in fact, the idea is that it's simple. It's a back-of-the-envelope-type equation that will help you understand whether or not it makes sense to delegate a task.

It's important that you complete this step, especially when you look at your list and see something you want to delegate, and the first thought that pops in your head is, It'll take too long. Will it? How do you know if you haven't crunched the numbers? So let's do it, shall we?

The delegation equation is about defining the time required to teach or explain what you need, as well as how long it will take you to review the work, and then comparing that to how long it actually takes you to do the work.

Delegation equation

If (T×N) > (R+O), then delegate.

If (T×N) < (R+O), then do not delegate.

(T)ime it takes to complete the task

(N)umber of times you'll do the task in the next three to twelve months

(R)equired time to teach the task

(O)utcomes review

SO IF IT TAKES 75 minutes to complete a task I do once every quarter, in one year, it'll take 300 minutes, or 5 hours (75 minutes × 4), of my time. If I can teach the task and review outcomes in less than 5 hours, then it's worth delegating.

For instance, if teaching the task takes 1 hour and reviewing it takes 1 hour (15 minutes each, 4 times a year), totaling 2 hours, it's a green light.

But if teaching takes 2 hours and reviewing takes 4 hours (1 hour, 4 times a year), totaling 6 hours, it's a no-go.

See more examples using the delegation equation at the end of the book (in the section Extra, Extra).

NOW, LIKE any good rule, this one also has an exception.
And here it is.
If (T×N) < (R+O), don't delegate unless...

- you hate the work,
- the work is robbing you of your energy, or
- you would make a bigger impact doing something else.

In these instances, while it might take you more time to delegate than it actually does to do the work, it's still better to delegate. Why? Tasks that rob you of your joy often take up more time than you think. There is the emotional buildup and wind-down time that comes with them. You also are less likely to be operating at the height of productivity while doing the work. If it's work you loathe, it's also likely there are other more valuable and impactful places you could be spending your time. In short, if you want to flourish, you need to release as many of the things that rob you of joy as you can even at the cost of an extra hour.

Activity

Run the delegation equation for your chosen task. Don't forget to apply the rule. If it makes sense to delegate, then move forward. If it doesn't, go back to your list and determine another task, define it, decide who will do it, and come back to do the math with this delegation equation.

Delegation equation:

If $(T \times N) > (R+O)$, then delegate.

If $(T \times N) < (R+O)$, then do not delegate.

(T)ime it takes to complete the task

(N)umber of times you'll do the task in the next three to twelve months

(R)equired time to teach the task

(O)utcomes review

At the end of the book (in the section Extra, Extra), I've provided additional examples for delegation equation activities for use at work, at home, and with your kids.

10

Discuss: Clearly Communicate the Task, Expectations, and Deadlines

ALRIGHT, MAMA, you are rocking and rolling here, and *so* close to effectively delegating your task. Be proud of yourself for what you've accomplished—we're over halfway through! Let's recap how far you've come.

1 You've determined what tasks to remove from your plate.
2 You've determined and articulated what a successful outcome is.
3 You have decided to whom you'll delegate.
4 You have done the math to ensure it makes sense.

Now it's time to plan out how you'll hand this task over.

I remember once I had wanted to delegate the setup of a large meeting to a team member. The meeting was for about forty-five people, including three to five different presenters, and would require meals provided for attendees. It was also a meeting we had quarterly. The person I wanted to delegate this to, let's call her Jan, had been to the meeting several times.

One day, at the end of a one-on-one where we had spent the majority of the time working through a work challenge she had, I quickly asked her to take on the setup of the meeting. She gladly agreed and I rushed off to my next meeting.

A couple of weeks later, about five weeks before the meeting, I asked for a progress update. Jan hadn't even started the work.

Now Jan was a very capable and valued employee, but she hadn't put together a meeting this complex before. When she said yes, she'd do it, I made the very poor assumption that she knew *what* to do. As it turned out, she didn't.

The biggest problem was that Jan didn't know what she didn't know. She had organized meetings before, and she had been to this meeting, but she was unclear on the steps required to pull off a meeting of this magnitude.

I cleared time the next afternoon to go through the various steps and discuss deadlines and the successful outcomes. I was very nervous about the timing. One of the most difficult things with a meeting this large was finding a space to hold it. It could take weeks to secure. Luckily, we were able to find a space and get the meeting together.

I had a true moment of freak-out and some real clarity that when it comes to effectively delegating, we have to take the time to clearly communicate the task, expectations, and deadlines and make sure the other person understands them.

It wasn't Jan's fault that she hadn't started the work; it was mine.

I had pitched the project over the fence to her, assuming she would catch it and run with it. I don't want you to end up in that situation.

AT HOME, I've faced the same kind of situation. I remember one time walking through the living room after a busy day, only to see clothes strewn all over the floor and an abandoned sock just lounging on the couch. I was so over it. I decided that my four-year-old needed to get more involved in picking up his clothes. Exasperated, instead of cleaning it up myself, I called him into the room.

"You've got a new responsibility, Mister. You need to pick up your clothes and put them in the hamper, so get to it."

Of course, there was some dramatic moaning, but he eventually started gathering the clothes and tossing them into the hamper. The next day, after changing into his playclothes, my son bounded off to play, leaving his dirty clothes in a heap. I called him back and told him to pick up his clothes again. Cue more moaning.

This cycle went on for a few days until I realized it wasn't just because he was four that I had to keep asking. It was also *how* I was asking him to do this.

I had a lightbulb moment and decided to switch up my approach. I sat him down at the kitchen table after his snack and walked him through what he needed to do, why it was important, when to do it, and how he'd know he was done (all the clothes in the hamper; nothing left on the floor). From then on, it was so much easier to remind him to pick up his clothes. Taking the time to explain things, even though he was only four, made a world of difference.

SO WHAT we are going to do now is make a plan to have your delegate take on the task you have determined.

Is your delegate a novice, expert, or someone in-between? Understanding this will help determine your approach to how you discuss the task, expectations, and deadlines.

For example, if you are handing the task over to an expert, you may need to write a brief, send a detailed email with the KPIs you created, or set up a fifteen-minute call. If you are working with a novice, you may need to prepare supporting materials in advance, spend an hour with them, or even set up recurring sessions to teach them what they need to know.

When will you meet?

When you're gearing up to delegate a task, one of the crucial steps is planning when you will meet with your delegate. This planning is essential for several reasons, and it can significantly impact the success of the task and the efficiency of your collaboration. Here's why you need to nail down that meeting time with a bit of sass.

First, scheduling a specific meeting time sets clear expectations for both you and your delegate. It ensures that both parties are prepared and focused, reducing the chances of miscommunication or last-minute surprises. When you establish a set time to meet, it signals to your delegate that this task is important and that you're invested in its success. This level of commitment can motivate your delegate to approach the task with the same level of seriousness and diligence. No more "I didn't know it was due" excuses!

Second, determining when to meet allows for better time management. It helps you allocate your time more effectively and ensures that the task receives the attention it needs without interfering with other responsibilities. For your delegate, knowing the meeting schedule helps them manage their workload and prioritize the delegated task accordingly. This mutual understanding of the timeline can prevent unnecessary delays and keep the project on track. Time is money, honey!

Key takeaway: Planning when to meet helps build trust and rapport. Regular interactions foster open communication and a better understanding of each other's working styles and expectations. This relationship-building aspect is crucial for long-term collaboration and can make future delegations smoother and more effective.

Where will you meet?

When you're ready to delegate a task, one crucial detail that can make or break your meeting is the location. Choosing the right place to meet with your delegate isn't just about convenience; it's about setting the stage for productive and effective communication. Here's why nailing down where you'll meet is so important.

The environment you choose for your meeting can significantly impact the tone and effectiveness of your discussion. A quiet, private space is ideal for detailed conversations where you need to share sensitive information or provide in-depth instructions. At work, this means booking a conference room for a project kickoff meeting to ensure your team can discuss plans without interruptions. At home, having a sit-down at the kitchen table after dinner might be the best place to explain to your partner how you'd like the yard work divided or to walk your teenager through their new chore schedule. Choosing the right atmosphere helps ensure that your delegate is comfortable and focused, making it easier to have a

When you establish a
set time to meet, it signals to
your delegate that this task
is important and that
you're invested in its success.

productive conversation. Forget the noisy break room or the living room with the TV blaring—pick a spot where you can get down to business!

Selecting a meeting location that minimizes distractions is key to maintaining focus. When you meet in a cluttered or busy environment, it's easy for both you and your delegate to get sidetracked. At work, avoid the break room for important meetings and instead opt for a quiet office space. At home, turn off the TV, and choose a quiet moment when the kids are asleep or occupied to discuss tasks with your partner. The fewer distractions, the more likely you are to stay on track and cover everything you need to discuss. After all, who needs interruptions when you're trying to get things done?

Accessibility is another critical factor in choosing a meeting location. You want to make sure the place you select is convenient for both you and your delegate. At work, this might mean choosing a conference room that's centrally located for all team members or opting for a virtual meeting if you have remote workers. At home, it might mean picking a spot that's comfortable for everyone involved, like the living room, where you can all sit down together. Picking a location that's easy to reach ensures that both parties arrive on time and are in the right mindset to have a productive meeting. Let's be real, nobody wants to trek across town or navigate a maze to get to a meeting.

Where you meet can also set the tone for the professionalism of your discussion. Meeting in a formal office or conference room underscores the importance of the task and conveys that you take the delegation seriously. It signals to your delegate that this is a professional commitment and that their role in the task is valued. For instance, discussing quarterly targets in a meeting room sets a different tone than chatting about it casually in the hallway. At home, while the setting might be more casual, choosing a specific time and place for your discussion, like a Sunday evening family meeting, shows that you value the task and the person's role in it. You want your delegate to know you mean business, even if you're sitting in your pajamas.

Lastly, choosing the right location ensures you have all the resources you need at your fingertips. If your meeting requires you and your delegate to review documents, a space with a large table and proper lighting is ideal. For presentations or demonstrations at work, a room equipped with the necessary technology, like a projector or a whiteboard, is essential. At home, if you're delegating tasks to your kids, having the chore chart, cleaning supplies, or whatever they need readily available can make the discussion and the actual task completion smoother. Ensuring that your meeting place has the required resources prevents interruptions and keeps the meeting running smoothly. No more scrambling for materials—be prepared and make it seamless.

Key takeaway: The location of your meeting plays a pivotal role in the success of your delegation process. It helps create the right atmosphere, minimizes distractions, ensures accessibility, sets a professional tone, and provides the necessary resources for a productive discussion. Whether you're delegating at work or at home, thoughtfully choosing where you'll meet can lay the groundwork for effective communication and successful task completion.

How long will you meet?

When it comes to delegating tasks, one often overlooked detail is the length of your meeting. Deciding how long you will meet with your delegate is crucial for ensuring the discussion is productive and efficient.

Let's be real, nobody likes a meeting that drags on forever. Determining the appropriate length of your meeting shows respect for everyone's time. At work, if you know the discussion will be short and sweet, schedule a quick fifteen-minute check-in. This keeps your team focused and prevents meeting fatigue. On the flip side, if you're planning a detailed project review, don't squeeze it into a thirty-minute slot. Give it the full hour it deserves to cover everything thoroughly without rushing.

At home, the same principle applies. If you need to delegate a simple chore to your partner or kids, a five-minute chat might suffice. However, if you're discussing a more involved task such as cleaning the pantry, you'll need to set aside more time to go over all the details. Respecting everyone's time keeps the process smooth and shows you value their contribution.

A well-timed meeting helps keep everyone on track. When you set a clear time frame, it encourages participants to stay focused and get to the point. This is especially important at work, where time is money. For example, if you're delegating a report, you might need a thirty-minute meeting to outline the key milestones and expectations. Keeping the meeting tight ensures you cover the essentials without veering off into unnecessary tangents.

At home, when delegating tasks to your kids, a short, focused meeting can work wonders. If you're asking them to clean their room, a quick ten-minute chat about what needs to be done and by when can be much more effective than a long-winded lecture. Keeping it brief and to the point helps them understand their responsibilities clearly without getting overwhelmed.

Determining how long you'll meet also helps ensure clarity and understanding. Rushing through a meeting because you didn't allocate enough time can lead to confusion and mistakes. For example, if you're delegating a complex task at work, such as a new marketing campaign, make sure you have enough time to explain the strategy, answer questions, and address any concerns. A rushed meeting can result in missed details and miscommunication.

At home, if you're teaching your teenager how to do laundry, a twenty-minute session might be necessary. You'll need time to walk them through sorting clothes, choosing the right settings, and explaining how to use the detergent. Giving yourself enough time to explain and demonstrate ensures they grasp the task fully and can do it correctly on their own.

Setting the right meeting length helps build trust and accountability. When you allocate sufficient time for a thorough discussion, it shows your delegate that you're serious about the task and their role in it. At work, this can mean the difference between a team that's engaged and one that's checked out. For instance, spending an hour at a project kickoff meeting ensures everyone is on the same page and committed to the project's success.

At home, spending adequate time to discuss responsibilities with your partner or kids can foster a sense of teamwork and accountability. If you're planning a family event, a well-timed meeting allows everyone to voice their opinions, assign tasks, and agree on deadlines. This collaborative approach strengthens your family's commitment to getting things done.

Finally, determining how long you'll meet helps avoid burnout. Long, unstructured meetings can drain energy and enthusiasm. By setting a clear time frame, you ensure that meetings are productive and leave everyone feeling energized rather than exhausted. At work, this means having a mix of short check-ins and longer, in-depth discussions as needed, maintaining a healthy balance.

At home, keeping meetings with your family short and sweet helps maintain harmony. If you need to delegate weekend chores, a quick ten-minute discussion over breakfast can set the plan for the day without eating into your family time. Balancing meeting lengths keeps everyone motivated and ready to tackle their tasks.

Key takeaway: Determining how long you will meet with your delegate is crucial for respecting time, staying focused, ensuring clarity, building trust, and avoiding burnout. Whether at work or at home, thoughtfully planning the length of your meetings can make all the difference in achieving successful delegation and maintaining a positive, productive atmosphere.

How often will you meet?

When it comes to delegating tasks, deciding how often you will meet with your delegate is just as crucial as the meeting itself. Regular check-ins can make the difference between a task that's completed successfully and one that derails. Here's why determining the frequency of your meetings is important.

Regular meetings help maintain momentum on the delegated task. At work, if you've assigned a long-term project, such as a six-month marketing campaign, having weekly or biweekly check-ins can keep the project moving forward. These consistent touchpoints ensure that any roadblocks are addressed promptly and that progress is continuously made. Think of it as keeping the engine running smoothly—frequent check-ins keep everything on track.

At home, maintaining momentum is just as vital. If you've tasked your teenager with keeping their room clean, a weekly review might be necessary. This regular check-in helps reinforce the habit and ensures that the task doesn't fall by the wayside. Keeping the frequency consistent reminds everyone that the task is ongoing and important.

Determining how often you'll meet also allows you to provide the necessary support and guidance. At work, if you're working with someone new to the task or project, more frequent meetings might be required initially. For instance, daily or every-other-day check-ins can help a new team member get up to speed and build confidence. As they become more comfortable with their responsibilities, you can scale back to weekly meetings.

At home, providing support is equally crucial. If your partner is taking on a new household chore, such as meal planning and cooking, frequent check-ins can be helpful. You might start with daily discussions to plan meals and shopping lists, gradually reducing the frequency as they get the hang of it. This approach ensures they feel supported and not left to figure everything out on their own.

Regular meetings foster accountability. When your delegate knows they have to report back on their progress, they're more likely to stay on top of their tasks. At work, setting a consistent meeting schedule, such as a weekly project review, keeps team members accountable and motivated to meet their deadlines. It creates a rhythm that everyone can rely on.

At home, the same principle applies. If your child knows they'll have a Saturday morning check-in about their chores, they're more likely to complete them on time. Regular meetings set clear expectations and help develop a sense of responsibility.

Determining the frequency of your meetings also allows for flexibility in adjusting and adapting as needed. At work, if you notice that the weekly meetings are too frequent and result in repetitive updates, you can switch to biweekly or monthly check-ins. Conversely, if you find that issues are

Without a clear definition of success and KPIs to measure it, you and your delegate are navigating without a map.

not being addressed quickly enough, you can increase the frequency. It's about finding the right balance that works for both you and your delegate.

At home, flexibility is just as important. If your initial plan of weekly check-ins with your partner about household tasks proves too frequent, you can adjust to biweekly meetings. On the other hand, if tasks are falling through the cracks, increasing the frequency can help get things back on track. Being adaptable ensures that the meeting schedule serves its purpose effectively.

Frequent meetings can also help build stronger relationships. At work, regular face-to-face time (or virtual face-to-face time) with your delegate fosters better communication and understanding. It helps you get to know each other's working styles and builds trust. These relationships can lead to a more cohesive and collaborative team environment.

At home, spending time regularly to discuss tasks and responsibilities can strengthen family bonds. Whether it's planning a family event or dividing household chores, regular check-ins provide opportunities to connect and collaborate. It reinforces the idea that everyone is in it together and contributes to a supportive home environment.

Lastly, determining the right frequency of meetings helps avoid overwhelm. Too many meetings can be as problematic as too few. At work, if team members feel bombarded with constant check-ins, it can lead to burnout and frustration. Striking the right balance ensures that meetings are productive and not burdensome.

At home, keeping the frequency reasonable ensures that check-ins are seen as helpful rather than a chore. Finding the sweet spot where meetings are frequent enough to be effective but not so frequent that they become a nuisance is key.

Key takeaway: Determining how often you will meet with your delegate is crucial for maintaining momentum, providing support, ensuring accountability, adjusting as needed, building strong relationships, and avoiding overwhelm. Whether at work or at home, thoughtfully planning the frequency of your meetings can significantly enhance the success of your delegation efforts and foster a positive, productive atmosphere.

What is success?

Without a clear definition of success and KPIs to measure it, you and your delegate are navigating without a map.

No one likes to be left guessing. Defining what success looks like provides clarity and direction for your delegate. At work, this means specifying exactly what the completed task should look like, how it should be executed, and what outcomes are expected. For example, if you're delegating the creation of a marketing report, success might be defined as a comprehensive document that includes analysis of key metrics, insights into performance, and actionable recommendations.

At home, defining success is just as important. If you're asking your teenager to clean their room, success might mean a tidy space with no clothes on the floor, a made bed, and dusted surfaces. Being clear about what you expect ensures that everyone is on the same page and knows exactly what they need to achieve.

KPIs are your best friends when it comes to measuring progress. They provide tangible, objective criteria to evaluate how well the task is being executed. At work, KPIs for a marketing campaign might include metrics like click-through rates, conversion rates, and return on investment. These indicators help you track whether the campaign is hitting its targets and where adjustments may be needed.

At home, KPIs can be just as useful. For instance, if you've delegated meal planning to your partner, KPIs could include staying within the weekly grocery budget, incorporating healthy options, and ensuring there's minimal food waste. These measurable outcomes help you gauge whether the task is being completed successfully and efficiently. So if you did not take the time to write out solid KPIs, go back to that part of the book in chapter 7 and do it (pretty please).

Another benefit of discussing clear success criteria and KPIs is that it helps identify issues early. When you walk through what success looks like, you give your delegate the opportunity to think through how they feel about the completing the task. It provides a chance to talk through what it takes to deliver successfully and lets you both get aligned on the final outcome.

Defining success and using KPIs ensure consistency and quality in task execution. At work, this means that every team member understands the standards they need to meet, leading to more uniform and high-quality outcomes. If you're delegating the creation of a series of reports, having clear success criteria and KPIs ensures that each report meets the same high standards, regardless of who completes it.

At home, setting these parameters ensures that tasks are done to your satisfaction every time. Whether it's cleaning, cooking, or managing household finances, clearly defined success criteria and KPIs help maintain a consistent level of quality. No more wondering if the job was done right—clear standards make it obvious.

Finally, defining success and using KPIs provide a basis for constructive feedback and continuous improvement. At work, regular reviews of KPIs allow you to provide specific feedback to your team members. If a project is falling short, you can discuss the areas that need improvement and develop a plan to get back on track.

At home, KPIs can be a great tool for providing feedback to your family. If your child's room-cleaning efforts aren't meeting the mark, you can discuss what needs to change and how they can do better next time. This approach not only helps improve performance but also fosters a positive environment for learning and growth.

Key takeaway: Defining what success looks like and using KPIs are essential for effective delegation. They provide clarity, measure progress, foster accountability, identify issues early, ensure consistency and quality, and facilitate feedback and improvement. Whether you're delegating tasks at work or at home, these tools help you achieve better outcomes and make the delegation process smoother and more successful.

When does this need to be done by?

Setting a deadline and discussing when a task needs to be completed is a critical aspect of effective delegation. Deadlines are not just about time management: they provide structure, accountability, and a sense of urgency that can drive performance. Here's why setting a deadline is essential and how to discuss it with your delegate, whether at work or at home.

Deadlines create a sense of urgency that motivates people to act. Without a specific time frame, tasks can easily fall by the wayside, overshadowed by more immediate concerns. At work, setting a deadline for a project—such as completing a marketing report by the end of the month—ensures that it gets prioritized among the many competing tasks. It helps your delegate focus their efforts and manage their time effectively.

Deadlines are not just about time management: they provide structure, accountability, and a sense of urgency that can drive performance.

At home, deadlines can be equally motivating. If you need your teenager to clean their room, telling them it needs to be done by Saturday morning provides a clear target. This urgency helps them understand the importance of the task and encourages them to get it done promptly. It turns a vague request into a concrete action plan.

Deadlines provide structure and clarity to the delegation process. They define the timeline for task completion and set clear expectations. At work, when delegating a task, you might say, "I need the draft of the marketing report by the fifteenth, so we can review it before the final submission on the thirtieth." This not only gives your delegate a clear time frame but also outlines the steps leading up to the final deadline.

At home, structure and clarity are just as important. If asking your partner to handle the grocery shopping, you could say, "Can you have the shopping done by Friday evening, so we have everything we need for the weekend?" This sets a clear time frame and helps avoid last-minute stress. Everyone knows what needs to be done and by when, which reduces ambiguity and confusion.

Setting a deadline enhances accountability. When a specific date or time is established for task completion, your delegate is more likely to take ownership and responsibility for meeting that deadline. At work, this means team members are held accountable for their deliverables, and there's a clear benchmark for evaluating performance. If a task isn't completed on time, it's easier to identify the issue and address it.

At home, deadlines hold family members accountable for their responsibilities. If your child knows they need to complete their homework by Sunday evening, it sets a clear expectation. If they don't meet the deadline, it becomes a learning opportunity to discuss time management and responsibility. Accountability fosters a sense of ownership and commitment to the task.

Deadlines facilitate planning and coordination. At work, they help you organize multiple tasks and projects, ensuring that everything is aligned and progressing smoothly. For example, if a team is working on a product launch, setting deadlines for each phase—research, development, marketing, and sales—ensures that everyone knows their role and the timeline. This coordination prevents bottlenecks and ensures timely delivery.

At home, deadlines help coordinate family activities and responsibilities. If you're planning a family trip, setting deadlines for booking flights, packing, and making final preparations ensures that everything is done in time. It helps avoid last-minute chaos and ensures a smooth and enjoyable experience. Planning and coordination are essential for keeping everything running like a well-oiled machine.

Deadlines are a powerful antidote to procrastination. Knowing that a task must be completed by a specific time pushes people to start and finish their work rather than put it off. At work, this means tasks are less likely to be delayed, and projects move forward steadily. If an employee knows they need to submit a proposal by Friday, they're less likely to procrastinate and more likely to plan their work accordingly.

At home, deadlines help prevent the "I'll do it later" syndrome. If your partner knows the garage needs to be cleaned out by the end of the month, they're more likely to tackle the task gradually rather than leaving it until the last minute. Deadlines provide a clear endpoint, reducing the temptation to delay and encouraging timely action.

Discussing deadlines with your delegate is crucial for ensuring they are realistic and achievable. Here's how to approach the conversation:

1 *Be clear and specific.* Clearly state when the task needs to be completed. Avoid vague timelines such as "soon" or "whenever you can." Instead, say, "I need this report by the end of the day on Friday."

2 *Explain the reason.* Explain why the deadline is important. Understanding the bigger picture can motivate your delegate to meet the deadline. For example, say, "We need the report by Friday, so we can review it over the weekend and present it to the client on Monday."

3 *Check availability.* Ensure that your delegate has the time and resources to meet the deadline. Ask if the proposed timeline is feasible and if they have any potential conflicts. This shows respect for their workload and promotes realistic planning.

4 *Set interim milestones.* For longer tasks, set interim deadlines or milestones to track progress. For instance, say, "Can you send me the first draft by Wednesday, so we have time for revisions before the final submission on Friday?"

5 *Offer support.* Let your delegate know that you're available to help if needed. You can help by providing additional resources, answering questions, or removing obstacles. For example, say, "If you need any data or have questions, feel free to reach out to me before Wednesday."

Key takeaway: Setting a deadline and discussing when a task needs to be done is a cornerstone of effective delegation. It creates urgency, provides structure, enhances accountability, facilitates planning, reduces procrastination, and ensures that tasks are completed on time. By clearly communicating deadlines and supporting your delegate, you set the stage for successful task completion and a more productive and harmonious environment, both at work and at home.

Activity

It's time to make your plan for discussing the next task you want delegated. Answer the questions above based on your own needs. In this discussion, you want to be as a clear as possible with what is expected of your delegate. Remember that definition of success and walk them through it. Be sure you include the following:

- The time in which the task should be accomplished
- What success looks like
- Why they are completing the task
- How it might help them

11

Discourse: Follow Up, Provide Guidance, and Evaluate Progress

JUST TWO MORE STEPS to do before you are ready to hand off your task. This next step is crucial to getting a successful outcome, and it's imperative that you plan for it now, before you hand off the task. This step is about creating a plan to ensure success through ongoing communication.

Most of the tasks you delegate will be completed over multiple steps or over time. To get a successful outcome, you have to determine when you'll check in on the progress. How much you trust the delegate, how often you have worked with them on that type of task in the past, and if they are a novice, expert, or in-between will help to determine your path to effective discourse.

Let's take the example of making the bed.

I would likely delegate this to my husband if we have a guest coming for a visit. The conversation may go something like this.

"Hey, babe, my aunt is coming on Saturday. I need you to help me get the house ready for her by making the bed no later than Friday evening. You know she is particular about the bed she sleeps in, so please be sure to tuck the sheet tight, smooth the comforter, and fluff the pillows. I appreciate you doing this. Making sure her sleeping space is correct will help reduce any potential drama. Plus, she'll get to see what a great man I married."

This request clearly shows what success is, and the steps to get there and when it needs to be done are clearly defined. But in order to ensure the bed is made properly, I may ask my husband to follow up with me. Knowing he's made a bed before, I likely won't ask him for a midpoint check-in. Instead, I might ask him to text me a photo when he's done, just so I know we are both ready for my aunt's arrival.

If we look at the meeting planning example in the last chapter, the conversation might be a bit different. In that case, here is what I did, when I finally took the time to sit with Jan, to ensure good ongoing communication.

- The weeks leading up to the meeting we met for ten minutes each Monday to go over the progress that was made.

- We set milestones, and I asked for email updates throughout the week after each milestone was reached.

- We set a day two weeks before the meeting to ensure every task was completed.

Planning in advance how you'll monitor success sets your delegate up for success and reduces your worry about the outcome.

LET'S TAKE an example of asking your six-year-old to help with sweeping the floor after dinner.

Define: I've defined success as all food and debris off the ground and in the trash.

Decide Who: I've decided that my six-year-old can help with this.

Do the Math: The first few tries are going to take a long time, but given the number of meals we'll have together over the course of our lives, it's worth the time investment.

Now that these three Ds have been set, I need to come up with a plan to determine the discourse and ensure success. That plan would consider his age and that he is a true novice. So here is what the plan would look like:

1 I would plan to proactively check in with him after he has started and observe what he is doing. If I see he needs some advice, I'll provide it. Where he has cleaned the floor well, I'll point it out, so he can see the good job he is doing and know what success looks like.

2 Then I'll reinforce that he is capable of doing the chore and remind him that after the kitchen is cleaned, we can do a fun activity.

3 I'll remind him that I'll be in the living room and that he can ask me for help if he gets stuck.

4 I will then tell him to come and get me as soon as he's done.

At the end of the book, you'll find a collection of scripts for delegating tasks at work, at home, and with your kids. Use this guide whenever you need a little extra support.

Now it's time to make your own discourse plan.

What are the key milestones in this task?

It bears repeating: you've got to be crystal clear on what success looks like and how to get there. Part of this clarity comes from understanding the key milestones as the task progresses. Knowing these milestones helps you figure out when to check on the task's progress and communicate your expectations to your delegate. Whether these milestones are super obvious or not so much depends on the task.

If they're obvious, great! Write them down so you can clearly communicate them, and let your delegate know when you'll check in. If they're not clear, try these three ideas:

1 *Close your eyes and visualize the work being completed.* As the work gets done, what are the transitional points along the way? For example, when making the bed, there's a transitional point when you go from adjusting the fitted sheet to putting on the top sheet. This is a milestone. Another example: creating a presentation. The switch from finishing a spreadsheet to creating a graph is a milestone. As you visualize the work, jot down each transitional moment. These are your milestones.

2 *Delegate defining the milestones.* Maybe you're not an expert in the task area, and that's ok! Explain the task and what success looks like to your delegate and ask them to define the milestones. This gets them involved early, leading to deeper engagement, and it gives you a chance to further ensure alignment on the path to success.

Knowing the key milestones helps you figure out when to check on the task's progress and communicate your expectations to your delegate.

3. *Delegate to an expert.* If you and your delegate are both in the dark about the milestones, find someone who has completed the task before and ask them to help you define the milestones.

You don't need to check in at every milestone (we'll talk about that next), but you do need to define them to clearly understand what needs to be done. Having the milestones written out and discussed not only helps ensure you and your delegate are aligned on the path to success, but also gives you a great map to follow when things go sideways.

For example, when making the bed, if the top sheet is bumpy, you can say, "Let's start from what happened with the fitted sheet." If the graph isn't a good representation, you can say, "Let's go back to the spreadsheet and find other ways to visually represent these numbers."

Do you need to review each milestone?

Milestones create the road map for how the work gets done, but not every milestone needs your eagle-eyed scrutiny. So how do you decide which ones to review? The key is to balance ensuring progress and giving your delegate the freedom to work their magic. Here's how you can decide which milestones to keep an eye on.

First, consider the complexity and importance of the milestone. Milestones that are crucial to the final outcome or involve a significant chunk of work are prime candidates for review. For instance, in making the bed, the transition from adjusting the fitted sheet to putting on the top sheet might seem minor, but if that fitted sheet isn't on right, the whole bed-making process can fall apart. Reviewing this milestone ensures the foundation is solid before moving on.

Second, think about the experience and reliability of your delegate. If they're new to the task or have had some hiccups in the past, it's smart to check in more frequently. On the flip side, if your delegate is a rock star with a proven track record, you can afford to be more hands-off. For example, when creating a presentation, if your delegate is a data visualization whiz, you might skip reviewing the shift from spreadsheet completion to graph creation. Instead, focus on the final presentation to make sure it hits all the right notes.

Third, assess the potential for errors or misunderstandings. Milestones that are prone to mistakes or critical to the task's success should be at the top of your review list. In our bed-making scenario, ensuring the top sheet is smooth and the comforter is perfectly spread is crucial for that pristine, hotel-like bed. Checking these milestones can prevent a bed-making disaster that leaves your guest unimpressed.

Lastly, consider the overall timeline and deadlines. If a milestone is close to the final deadline, it's essential to review it to catch any last-minute issues that could derail the entire project. In creating a presentation, the milestone where the final draft is compiled is vital. Reviewing this ensures that all elements come together seamlessly and that there's enough time to make any necessary tweaks before the big day.

Key takeaway: Deciding which milestones to review involves evaluating the complexity and importance of the task, experience of the delegate, potential for errors, and proximity to the deadline. By thoughtfully selecting which milestones to review, you ensure the task progresses smoothly while empowering your delegate to take ownership of their work. This approach not only enhances the quality of the final outcome, but also fosters trust and growth within your team and family.

How will you review the milestone progress?

For the milestones you need to review, having a strong plan is key. A well-thought-out review plan ensures that you stay on top of progress and maintain the quality of work without micromanaging. Here's how to craft a solid review plan using the examples of making the bed and creating a presentation.

First, determine the frequency and method of your reviews. Decide how often you'll check in on each milestone and the best way to conduct these reviews. For making the bed, you might choose to do a quick visual check after each significant step: adjusting the fitted sheet, putting on the top sheet, and arranging the comforter. This could be as simple as a quick glance to ensure everything is neat and tidy. For creating a report, you might schedule regular progress meetings or request updates via email or a shared document. For instance, after finishing the spreadsheet, have your delegate send you the data to review before they move on to creating graphs.

Next, establish clear criteria for what constitutes a successful milestone. Define what success looks like at each stage, so your delegate knows exactly what you're looking for. In the bed-making example, success for the fitted sheet stage means it's smooth and tightly tucked with no wrinkles. For the top sheet, it should be evenly spread with the edges aligned. When arranging the comforter, it should be centered and fluffed. For the presentation, success for the finished spreadsheet might mean all data is accurate and formatted correctly. For the graph creation stage, ensure the graphs are clear, correctly labeled, and visually appealing.

Then, communicate your plan and expectations to your delegate. Make sure they understand when and how you'll be reviewing their work, and what criteria you'll be using to evaluate it. For the bed-making task, let your delegate (whether it's your partner or your kid) know that you'll be checking each step to ensure the bed is made to your standards. For the report, inform your delegate that you'll be reviewing the spreadsheet data before they move on to creating graphs, and then checking the final presentation to ensure it meets all objectives.

Finally, be consistent with your reviews and provide constructive feedback. Stick to your review schedule and use each check-in as an opportunity to give praise for what's done well and guidance on what can be improved. When checking the bed-making progress, praise a well-tucked sheet and offer tips if something is amiss. For the report, acknowledge accurate data entries and provide suggestions for any corrections or improvements needed in the graphs. Consistent, constructive feedback helps reinforce good practices and corrects issues early on, ensuring a smoother path to the final outcome.

Key takeaway: By planning your milestone reviews thoughtfully, you create a structured yet flexible framework that ensures quality without stifling your delegate's autonomy. This approach keeps the task on track, builds your delegate's skills and confidence, and ultimately leads to a successful, polished final result.

HERE'S WHY these questions matter and how to rock your follow-ups.

What are the key milestones in this task?
Why it's important: Identifying key milestones helps you break the task into bite-sized pieces and sets clear checkpoints. This way you can track progress and squash issues before they blow up.

Be consistent with your reviews and provide constructive feedback.

How to do it: List out the major steps or deliverables. For instance, if you've delegated planning an event, milestones might include nailing down a venue, sending out invites, and locking in guest RSVPs.

Do you need to review each milestone?
Why it's important: Knowing which milestones need your eagle-eyed review keeps you in the loop on critical parts without micromanaging every little detail. It ensures quality control without driving you (or them) crazy.

How to do it: Decide which milestones are crucial for you to check. In the event planning example, you might need to review the final guest list but not every potential venue.

How will you review the milestone progress?
Why it's important: Figuring out how to review each milestone keeps communication clear and follow-ups efficient. It sets expectations for updates and helps everyone stay on their A game.

How to do it: Pick the best method for each milestone. Here are some options.

- Read a report: Perfect for detailed updates where you need the nitty-gritty in writing
- Get a photo: Great for visual tasks, like seeing the venue setup
- Check a spreadsheet: Ideal for tracking data or progress, like keeping tabs on the budget
- Have a meeting: Perfect for tackling complex issues or brainstorming
- Get an email update: Quick and dirty for confirming a task is done

Example: Planning an event

Here's one example of how this process plays out in real life.

Key milestones
- Secure a venue
- Send out invitations
- Confirm guest attendance

Review needed
- Secure a venue (heck, yes)
- Send out invitations (nope)
- Confirm guest attendance (you bet)

Review method
- Secure a venue: Have a meeting to discuss options and make the final call
- Confirm guest attendance: Check a spreadsheet with guests' RSVP status

By answering these questions, you set a clear path for follow-ups, ensuring everything stays on track and meets your high standards. This approach not only helps you manage tasks efficiently, but also gives your delegate a sense of responsibility and accountability.

Keep this plan handy as you'll need to share it when you discuss your task.

12

(Happy) Dance: Celebrate Your Win!

DELEGATING ISN'T EASY, but you are going to do it. When you successfully delegate, you win and so does your delegate. Every success deserves some level of celebration. Every success should be recognized.

How are you going to celebrate the win for your delegate? It could be a high five, a pat on the back, an email expressing gratitude, or something more.

How are you going to celebrate the win for you? It could be a high five in the mirror, a mani-pedi, a nap, a positive affirmation, or more.

Below is a list of ideas, big and small, to help you think about how to celebrate.

You are on your way to finding more time in your life and to flourishing.

- *Cook your favorite meal.* If you are someone who loves to cook, go ahead and treat yourself to your favorite meal. Bonus tip: If you can get all those ingredients delivered so you don't have to go to the grocery store, you are winning twice with delegation.

- *Upgrade yourself.* If you normally go to the spa for a mani-pedi, get the upgraded treatment. Go ahead and splurge on that extra foot massage or paraffin treatment that you've been eyeballing. If you don't normally get your nails done, give it a whirl.

- *Have a grown-up slumber party.* Take a long weekend with the girls. If you can't do a full long weekend, do a staycation at a city near you or in a neighborhood next to yours with your girlfriends. You can rent a hotel, have room service, paint each other's nails, watch movies, and drink wine.

- *Make it a party for one.* Do the above but by yourself. Taking alone time is a great way to reward yourself. Go ahead and book a staycation for yourself. Try booking a Friday evening and then sleep in on Saturday, so you can be home in time for lunch with the kids. Still, having a Friday evening to yourself with the ability to sleep in and get room service will make a world of difference.

- *Read a book.* Take a trip to your local bookstore or library and get that book you've been eyeballing and then take some time to read it.
- *Treat yourself to pretty, pretty things.* Buy yourself something pretty. If you're into shiny, go for jewelry. If you're into soft, get some cashmere. Get yourself something nice and don't feel bad about it—you deserve it.
- *Enjoy the view.* Take the long way home and enjoy the view as you go.
- *Work out.* Take an exercise class that you've been meaning to sign up for. Try a barre class, a fancy cycling class, or a new yoga studio.
- *Say cheers.* Go to happy hour with some of your best colleagues.
- *Learn a new skill.* Take some time to learn a new skill. Whether it's painting, rock climbing, or macramé, take a class.

Activity

Now it's time to plan your celebration. Answer the following:

- How will you celebrate your delegate's accomplishments?
- How will you celebrate that you successfully delegated? (And yes, Mama, you do deserve to celebrate yourself for this!)

Delegation readiness quiz

Yassssss! You've done it. You've created a plan to leverage the strategic art of delegation for your task. You have two last actions to take and then it's time to celebrate with a cocktail.

Take the delegation test.

I've created a little test to help you make sure that you are really, truly ready to delegate your task. As you get better and better at delegating, you'll find yourself completing many of the 7 Ds in your head. This test is a surefire way to make sure you don't skip any steps. So take it now, print it out (from my website at thesavvyworkingmom.com/tookit), and hang it on your fridge or in your office, or carry it in your purse to make sure you are prepared every time you delegate.

Take this quiz, and if you answer no to any of the questions, figure out how you can make it a yes, or don't delegate.

- Do you have a clear and defined successful outcome in mind?
- Will you have the time to explain the task and, if needed, to teach someone how to complete the task?
- Do you have time to follow up and check in on your delegate's progress?

If you got all yeses, then it's time for you to delegate! Woot woot, and congrats. You are on your way to finding more time in your life and to flourishing.

Go ahead and kick-start your delegation discussion. Whether you need to set a meeting, send an email, or make a phone call, do it now. Once that's done, it's time to celebrate!

Cheers to you!

Woot woot! You did it! I'm so proud of you. I know it's not easy to delegate. I also know that it can be hard to stay on this delegation path. Don't worry about that right now. The next part of this book has everything you need to keep your time and energy focused on the things that will help you shine and flourish. So let's take a moment to recognize you with a toast.

Here's to you, the ultimate delegation diva! You're conquering your to-do list with flair, paving the way for more peace, fulfillment, and even a cocktail or two. Cheers to your savvy delegation skills and open calendar!

Now I know you might be thinking I'm going to suggest a champagne drink for your toast, but to me, all that hard work calls for something a little stronger. This next drink, the Boulevardier, is one of my go-tos when I'm looking for something classy that also gets the party started.

If you've ever heard of a negroni, this is basically the same drink except you swap the gin in the negroni for whiskey. It's a delicious, easy sipper that is served in a coupe. And who doesn't feel celebratory when drinking from a coupe?

BOULEVARDIER

Ingredients

1½ ounces bourbon or rye whiskey

1 ounce sweet vermouth

1 ounce Campari

Orange peel, for garnish

Instructions

1. Fill a mixing glass with ice.
2. Add the bourbon or rye whiskey, sweet vermouth, and Campari.
3. Stir well until chilled, about 30 seconds.
4. Pour the mixture into a chilled coupe glass.
5. Garnish with an orange peel.
6. Serve and celebrate your newfound skill of delegation!

13

Staying on the Prioritization and Delegation Path

L IFE IS LIKE a symphony, a dynamic masterpiece, that is both beautiful and ever-changing. Your not-for-me-to-do list isn't set in stone. As you prioritize and delegate tasks and tick them off (woo-hoo!), new ones will inevitably arise. I want to be sure that as your list changes, it creates order, not overwhelm.

It's all too easy to slip back into old habits when life gets hectic. But fear not, I've got the tools you need to prevent that from happening. In this section of the book, we'll delve into how to maintain and evolve your not-for-me-to-do list, ensuring that your time and energy are invested where they matter most. Our goal? To focus on activities that truly make a difference, bring joy, and maybe even leave room for a well-deserved cocktail or two.

Remember, prioritization and delegation are skills, and practice makes perfect. Along the way, you may encounter some bumps in the road. The first tool I'll give you is a list of challenges people face when delegating and how to overcome them. From there we'll dive into how to say "no" (without feeling guilty) and how to keep your time and energy focused on the areas that will bring you joy and move the needle in your life.

Top three delegation challenges and how to handle them

I know I've said this a lot, but I'll say it one more time: Delegation is a skill. It takes time to develop skills. I know you can get really good at delegation with practice. As you delegate certain tasks from your not-for-me-to-do list, you may hit some roadblocks. You might find yourself unsuccessfully delegating—don't worry, that's normal. It's not failing; it's a chance to hone your delegation skills.

One thing my grandma used to say to me is "failing to plan is planning to fail." So let's take a look at the top three challenges you may face along the way as you start to delegate and prepare to handle them before they even occur.

1. *Lack of trust.* After delegating a task to someone, you may find yourself second-guessing them and having trouble trusting them.

    Solution: Review your discourse plan. Do you have enough milestones in place? Do you have enough check-ins? Are the types of check-ins you are doing (emails, meetings, reports, etc.) meeting your needs? Should you change how often or when you review, or the format for reviewing progress? Make updates to your discourse plan to ensure you have enough communication to trust your delegate.

2 **The delegate can't deliver.** After delegating a task to someone, you may find that they can't actually deliver successfully for you.

Solution: Figure out what the problem is and course correct. Is it that they don't have the skill? If so, can you teach them? If you can't teach them, is there someone else that you can delegate to? Is it that they don't have the time? If so, can you help them eliminate, pause, or delegate other tasks so that they can make the time? Is it that they misunderstood the assignment? If so, can you clarify it for them?

3 **Difficulty letting go.** After delegating a task to someone, you may find it difficult to relinquish control and trust another person to complete the task.

Solution: First, reaffirm what your successful outcome is and focus on that. If that doesn't help, change the tasks you are delegating. Rather than delegating your biggest task, start with smaller ones. This will let you practice letting go of control. As you get more comfortable, you can gradually increase the complexity and scope of delegated tasks.

Another helpful tool when you are struggling to let go is role-play. Take a moment to role-play handing off the task. Role-playing is most effective when you can bring someone in to play the delegate. But if not, no worries, just complete the role-play in your head.

- Imagine delegating the chosen task. Visualize yourself communicating effectively with the person you're delegating to.
- Mentally go through the steps of sharing your delegation plan, ensuring clarity and understanding. Imagine what

questions or pushbacks they may have. Picture yourself answering them with confidence and clarity.

- Take a moment to reflect on the role-play exercise. Consider any challenges you encountered during the mental simulation and what you learned from it.

Top three prioritization challenges and how to handle them

Once you've cleared your not-for-me-to-do list, you'll probably still have a hefty list of tasks you want to accomplish—it can be tough to prioritize these tasks. When I'm figuring out what to do, I like to put tasks into three categories, adding an asterisk (*) for tasks I enjoy:

1 Urgent
2 Important
3 Other

The asterisk is for tasks I want to do or I enjoy doing. I've added the asterisk because identifying tasks that make my heart sing, like making dinner, holding my baby, or presenting to a large audience, helps me mentally prepare for what I'm about to do. Depending on the day, if my energy is low, I might start with an urgent task that doesn't have an asterisk, knowing that as my energy dwindles, it'll be easier to get through the urgent or important tasks that do have an asterisk.

Here are some key differences between urgent and important tasks:

Urgent: Urgent tasks are time-sensitive and driven by external factors such as deadlines or emergencies.

Important: Important tasks support progress toward your personal and professional long-term goals. These are tasks that

Remember, prioritization
and delegation
are skills, and practice
makes perfect.

need to be completed, like having 1:1 meetings, taking that language course, or reviewing a board presentation, so you can live a life you love.

Our brains can struggle to tell the difference between what's important and what is urgent. This is one reason important things sometimes feel urgent when they really are not. Another big reason is because someone else has told you they are important or urgent based on their needs or understanding and not yours.

Something that helps me to sort through all my tasks and prioritize then into urgent/important is the Eisenhower Matrix. This two-by-two matrix was popularized by business writers such as Stephen Covey, but it's most often attributed to former US president Dwight D. Eisenhower, who famously said, "I have two kinds of problems: the urgent and the important. The urgent are not important, and the important are never urgent."[1] Although he was quoting a former college president he knew personally, Eisenhower got the credit.

	URGENT	NOT URGENT
IMPORTANT	**DO** THIS	**DECIDE** THIS
NOT IMPORTANT	**DELEGATE** THIS	**DELETE** THIS

Whether something is urgent or important is primarily driven by whether it has an imminent deadline. Urgent matters must be handled immediately. If possible, they should be dealt with today. Important tasks may have a deadline, but it's typically further. When important tasks are left to linger too long, like preparing that science project, they become urgent.

Remember, just because someone says something is urgent doesn't mean it is. Consider what might happen if you don't meet the deadline. If the consequences are insignificant, is the task truly so urgent that it needs to usurp every other task on your to-do list? Just because your toddler is demanding apple juice "right now" doesn't mean it's actually urgent. Similarly, just because a coworker says they need that report by tomorrow doesn't make it true. If it's unclear why the other person has set their deadline, ask:

"Toddler, are you dying?"

"Colleague, what's driving the quick turnaround?"

When you start to feel overwhelmed with what you need to accomplish on any given day or week, whip out the matrix and fill it in. Focus on the urgent and then the important. As new tasks come to you, be sure that everything you are considering spending time and energy on isn't something that needs to be put on your not-for-me-to-do list.

If you have trouble figuring out where to put a task on the matrix, ask yourself some questions. Am I doing this for me or someone else? Is this adding value to my life? Is this aligned with my goals? What happens if I don't do this thing today or this week? Do I really have to be the one to do it or can I delegate?

Mama, don't forget, you can't do everything, and trying to do it all will be your downfall. Ensure you are regularly eliminating tasks and moving things to your not-for-me-to-do list.

Mama, don't forget,
you can't do everything,
and trying to do
everything is keeping
you down.

Even with the matrix, you might still find prioritizing challenging. Don't worry, just like delegation, prioritization is a skill. And even the best of us fails sometimes. So let's go back to what my grandma said and make a plan to help us through our prioritization slumps. The following are the top three challenges I've seen when it comes to prioritizing and how to overcome of them.

1. *Overwhelming task list.* With a seemingly endless list of tasks, it can be hard to decide what to tackle first.

   Solution: Revisit each task and double-check that you are the one who needs to complete it. Then try to break down your tasks into smaller, manageable chunks. Maybe part of what you need to do must happen today, but the rest can wait until later in the week or even next month. (Please note the clean but unfolded pile of laundry in the basket.) If that doesn't work, then take five minutes and write down the three things you must do today, and focus on completing those or ensuring they are set up. By set up, I mean in place to happen. One thing I have to do every day is feed my family, but some days I just can't cook. Prescheduling a food delivery means I've completed that task and can move on. Another way to ensure something is set up is to block time on your calendar. Say I know I need to finish a presentation but can't until I get a certain report. I'll block the time on my calendar later in the day to finish the presentation after the report is due. When I block the time on my calendar, the task is out of my mind, and I can move on to the next thing. When the calendar notification pops up, I respect it and work on that task. Once those tasks are done, write the next three things you need to do and keep that process going until you finish what you need to do. The next morning revisit your list and see if on this new day, certain things seem urgent or you have more clarity on how to prioritize. Sometimes a good night's sleep is the answer.

2. *Difficulty setting boundaries.* When it comes to prioritizing, being concerned about how someone may feel if you don't prioritize their task may result in your putting their needs before your own. Or you have trouble putting your life and goals first.

Solution: Learn to set clear boundaries. Revisit your goals and why you have them. Remind yourself what you want out of life and that you deserve to have it. Then look at your list and ask yourself, Am I prioritizing others' needs over mine? Why? Refocus your energy on what you need to manage and where you want to shine.

3. *Lack of clear goals.* You must have clear goals. We talked about this before, so I don't want to sound like a broken record. But without clear goals, it's challenging to determine what's most important.

Solution: Revisit the section in chapter 6 on the nine areas of life and do the work to get clear on what you want and how you know you'll have achieved it.

BONUS TIP (who doesn't like a little something on the house?):

Procrastination. Sometimes, even when you know your priorities, you might still procrastinate on important tasks.

Solution: We procrastinate for a lot of different reasons. One of the reasons may be that we are exhausted or burned out, especially as women with so much on our plates. Check in with yourself and your mental health if you need more than this book. Talk to a therapist—put it at the top of your to-do list. Seriously, put this book down right now and set that appointment.

Cheers to overcoming challenges!

Choosing to delegate can be scary. I want to commend you for believing in yourself and being brave. It seems that at this time, downing a little liquid courage is the right thing to do, so I want to share with you a variation on an old fashioned I like to call Happy Accident. It's a powerful drink that is a little larger than most.

I came up with it doing what mamas do. No, not wine o'clock-ing as soon as the kids go to bed. Innovating! One night, yes, after the kids were in bed, I was set on making a drink with bourbon, lemon, and sugar. Well, I started pouring and realized I had only a smidge of bourbon left. That gave me two options, make a mini old fashioned or get creative. A mini-drink was of no interest to me, so I got creative. I had a bottle of apple brandy and thought, I'll give mixing sweet dark liquor with sweet dark liquor a go. So I added the apple brandy. It was delicious. When my husband asked, "How'd you come up with this?" I said, "It's a happy accident," and the name stuck. When I think about that happy accident, I also think about how we sometimes need to flex as we delegate. If things are not going exactly to plan, don't fret; don't hesitate to look around and see what tools and resources you have, then apply them to get the outcome you desire.

Note

1 Dwight D. Eisenhower, "Address at the Second Assembly of the World Council of Churches," Northwestern University, August 19, 1954, Evanston, IL.

HAPPY ACCIDENT

Ingredients

1½ ounces bourbon

1½ ounces apple brandy

¾ ounce fresh lemon juice

1½ tablespoons sugar

Lemon peel or thinly sliced apple wedge, for garnish (optional)

Instructions

1. Fill a cocktail shaker with ice cubes.
2. Add the bourbon, apple brandy, lemon juice, and sugar to the shaker.
3. Shake well until the mixture is thoroughly chilled, about 15 to 20 seconds.
4. Strain the cocktail into a chilled glass filled with ice.
5. Optionally, garnish with a lemon peel or an apple slice.
6. Serve and revel in your newfound courage to delegate.

14

The Grace and Joy Morning Routine

HIGH FIVE, MAMA! You have done a lot of work! I hope you have taken time to celebrate along the way. Now I want to talk to you about how to make this all stick. The secret is a morning routine.

Before you go rolling your eyes or close the book, it's not just any morning routine. It's my patented Grace and Joy routine designed specifically for working moms.

What if you could easily wake up ready to slay the day at home and at work? Using my routine, in as little as six minutes, you can set yourself up for stress-free success—and you don't even have to wake up earlier. Let me walk you through how I crafted my morning routine.

I've always been an early bird, mainly because after 10:00 p.m., I'm about as useful as a screen door on a submarine—unless you count mixing cocktails and doing the wobble as productive tasks. So when faced with goals that demanded more time than my regular day allowed, I started setting my alarm earlier and earlier. Before my wedding, I was hitting the gym at 5:00 a.m. And when I launched my blog, pre-delegation era, I was up at 4:30 a.m., chasing those creative dreams. Early mornings were my secret weapon.

Then came baby number two. Our boys might look like two peas in a pod with their matching curly hair and blue eyes, but when it came to sleep, they were on completely different wavelengths. For three years, it felt like a tag-team wrestling match: when one slept soundly, the other was up for a midnight party. And to add to the chaos, I welcomed my second bundle of joy in May 2020, right as the airline industry, in which I worked, was seeing its biggest challenge ever from the COVID-19 pandemic. Balancing home and work life was like juggling chain saws while riding a unicycle.

Amidst the madness, I knew I needed a lifeline to keep me focused on what truly mattered, to shine in the areas that counted, and to move the needle forward. But my old morning routine wasn't cutting it anymore. Waking up even earlier wasn't an option—I was already running on fumes.

At that point, I knew I could use more grace and joy in my life, and I bet you can too. I mean, who couldn't? Knowing this, I created the Grace and Joy morning routine to allow for just that, a little more grace and a lot more joy even when you can't wake up earlier. It's actually an acronym, and when you complete these actions within the first ninety minutes of your day you are bound to slay.

Why ninety minutes? Because life happens. Waking up before the kids at 4:30 a.m. to complete a morning routine isn't possible for most of us. And once the kids are up, anything is bound to happen. So spreading out these key steps to a great day across the first ninety minutes of your day is not only life-changing, but also realistic.

Grace and Joy

- **G**et hydrated
- **R**econnect with your body
- **A**ccept the moment
- **C**onjure the future
- **E**xpress gratitude
- **J**ust pick one
- **O**wn your mama
- **Y**ield potential

Let's dive into how to do each one. At the end of the book, I've provided a lot more ideas for developing your routine, specific to the time you have each day. Refer to this guide any time you want a helping hand.

Get hydrated and choose you!
The first thing to do each morning is choose to hydrate. When you choose to make hydration your first task, you are not only doing something good for your body, but also giving yourself the signal that you matter and that you will choose you first. The many benefits of hydrating are listed in the section Extra, Extra, and you can get all these benefits from a little hydration first thing in the morning. Here's how to make sure it happens: set some water by your bed each night. You can do this a few different ways:

1. Fill a reusable water bottle the night before and set it on your nightstand.
2. Store a filled water bottle under your bed, so you always have a spare.
3. Get a pretty carafe and keep a gallon of water near your bed for easy refills.
4. If you're not a fan of plain water, make it fancy by adding flavor or fruit, unsweetened tea, or even Crystal Light.

Choose hydration and choose yourself, because you deserve to start your day feeling fantastic!

Reconnect with your body
Some people might call it exercise, but I call it moving with intention. Our bodies carry so much of our energy and emotion. It's important to reconnect your mind and body after a night of sleep. This morning ritual not only improves cognitive function, emotional well-being, and physical health, but also sets a positive tone for facing daily challenges with resilience and mindfulness.

The great news is that this intentional movement doesn't have to be a ninety-minute high-intensity interval training workout (though it can be if you're into that and have the time). Simply stretching for three minutes can do the trick. The important part is that you move with the intention of feeling your body. By embracing the art of moving with intention, you unlock a myriad of benefits that sets a positive tone for your day and empowers you to navigate life's challenges with ease and peace.

Accept the moment

In the hustle and bustle of our daily lives, it's easy to overlook the importance of taking a moment for ourselves. We rush through our mornings, checking off tasks on our to-do lists, but how often do we truly pause to connect with our inner selves? In this fast-paced world, finding time for self-reflection, stillness, and inner peace can seem like a daunting task. However, the benefits of incorporating morning silence into our routines are profound and far-reaching.

Now that you've had some time to hydrate and move with intention, it's time to take a moment to be with yourself. Whether you choose to meditate, pray, or simply sit in silence, this practice is all about connecting with your inner self. It might sound easy, but for many of us, it can be a challenging endeavor. I remember when I first started this practice; I was always on the go and being still and alone with my thoughts felt like an alien concept. But let me assure you, it was worth every effort.

You don't need to commit to hours of meditation or solitude. Start with as little as sixty seconds and gradually work your way up to five minutes if you can. If even that feels daunting, begin with just thirty seconds and add fifteen seconds every other day. It's a journey, and you can tailor it to suit your comfort level. Set an alarm on your phone for the designated time, close your eyes, and begin to breathe.

As you breathe in and out, aim for a count of eight seconds for each inhalation and exhalation. This rhythmic breathing will help center your mind and body. Pay attention to how it feels to inhabit your body at this moment. Notice the pace of your breathing and observe if any areas of your body feel particularly relaxed or tense. Sitting with yourself, in silence, is a crucial step in ensuring you are setting yourself up for success in the day ahead.

The first thing to do each morning is choose to hydrate.

Taking this crucial step to be with yourself in the morning is necessary to living a life filled with joy. It's a small investment in yourself that yields immeasurable rewards. So make time for this practice, even if it's just for thirty seconds. Embrace the silence, connect with your inner self, and set the stage for a day brimming with positivity and purpose. Your well-being and joy are worth every moment of morning silence.

Conjure the future

Let's sprinkle some magic into your morning routine, shall we? Sometimes I wish I had a crystal ball to sneak a peek into the future! But guess what? We've got something even cooler—the superpower of visualization! It's like dreaming with your eyes wide open. You see, we're not just passengers on this life journey; we're the pilots, shaping our destinies through the choices we make and how we react to life's twists and turns. Visualization, my friend, is the ultimate tool that can turn your dreams into reality. Visualizing helps us to connect to our goals and the steps we need to achieve them.

Conjuring the future is like painting your own masterpiece. It's about taking a moment to create a mental canvas of your heart's desires, allowing your mind and body to dance to the rhythm of having those dreams come true. And here's the secret sauce—feeling! Feeling is the magic ingredient. As you dive into this adventure, shut your eyes and let the magic begin.

Here's how to do it. Close your eyes and picture yourself living your dream life. Imagine everything you wrote down in chapter 6 has come true. The relationship you have with your kids is exactly what you want, your career is where you want it to be, your love life is amazing—you've achieved all your hopes and dreams.

Picture what it feels like when all your goals are accomplished. What are you doing? What clothes are you wearing? What is your day like? Dive into the emotions of joy and pride and gratitude, and let them envelop you in the warm glow of achievement.

If you try to do this and feel stuck or need a little inspiration, you can create a vision board and look at that. Creating a vision board just means putting images that inspire you (such as pictures you cut out from a magazine or print from an online source) onto a piece of paper.

If you're currently living in a cozy two-bedroom townhouse but secretly dream of a sprawling five-bedroom mansion, find a photo of a home you'd love to live in and put it on your vision board. Then when you are visualizing your dream home, dive deep into what it would be like to live there. What does it smell like? Where are your kids playing? Are you hosting epic gatherings in that marvelous space? How have you decorated? Imagine everything down to the last throw pillow.

Or perhaps your heart longs for a deeper connection with your children. Put up a photo of them from a great day you had. And when you visualize, picture this: your phone buzzes, and it's your kids calling from college, not because they need money (phew!) but because they're itching for a heart-to-heart chat with their fabulous mama. What are you discussing? How does that warm connection make you feel?

Taking a moment in the morning to visualize your success is a critical part of ensuring you focus your energy and actions through the day.

Express gratitude

Cultivating a sense of gratitude each morning can be a transformative practice that brings a multitude of benefits to your life. It's a simple yet powerful way to start your day on a positive note, and there are various methods to incorporate gratitude into your morning routine. The key is to choose the approach that resonates with you the most.

For someone like me, expressing gratitude out loud is the preferred method. Each morning, I vocalize the things I'm grateful for. I say, "I'm so grateful for my kids' health," "I'm thankful to have a supportive husband," "I appreciate my own health," and so on. As I utter these words, I allow the feelings of gratitude to well up inside me, filling me with positivity and appreciation.

Another effective way to practice gratitude is through writing. You can keep a gratitude journal or jot down your blessings on a Post-it that you carry with you throughout the day. Alternatively, consider sharing your gratitude with someone else, whether by sending a text message to a friend or partner or by making it a habit to share things you're thankful for at the breakfast table. Sharing your gratitude is a powerful way to inspire others to embrace this practice too.

When it comes to the content of your gratitude, the possibilities are endless. You can focus on things happening in the present or recall experiences from the past.

- People in your life: Express gratitude for the people you cherish, such as your children, family, or friends.
- Experiences you've had: Reflect on past experiences that have enriched your life, such as living in another country or traveling.
- Things you have: Be thankful for the material possessions that bring comfort and convenience to your life, such as your air conditioner or cell phone.

The act of expressing your gratitude in the morning can be tailored to your preferences. You can choose to speak your gratitude, write it down, or share it with others. If you haven't already, consider creating a gratitude list—a compilation of all the things you're thankful for. Keep it in a convenient place, such as in your purse or on your nightstand. This written record serves as a powerful reminder during challenging times when it may be difficult to recall what you're grateful for. It rekindles that warm and positive feeling within you.

Personally, I keep my gratitude list in the back of my agenda. Whenever something wonderful happens, I make a note of it. Then, on those tough days when I need a boost of positivity the most, I simply open my agenda and revisit those moments. It serves as a beautiful reminder that life is full of goodness and that I've been fortunate.

Another creative way to practice gratitude is to maintain a gratitude jar. Whenever you feel grateful for something, write it down on a slip of paper and place it in the jar. Later, when you need a dose of positivity, you can draw a slip and relive a joyful memory.

Whether you choose to practice gratitude for sixty seconds or dedicate thirty minutes to it, the duration is entirely up to you and can be adjusted based on your morning routine. The important thing is to embrace this practice as a way to start your day with a positive mindset and an open heart.

Just pick one

Imagine a world where you don't feel like you're drowning in a sea of endless to-dos. Instead, picture yourself confidently steering your ship toward the shores of your dreams, one task at a time. It's all about picking just one, yes, just one action, and watching your progress soar.

In our busy lives filled with daily hustle and bustle, it's easy to get caught up in the chaos and forget what truly matters to us. That's where the magic of this practice comes in.

Following the Grace and Joy routine each morning is your secret sauce for living your dreams.

Every morning, you get to play the game of Pick Your Top Priority. Choose the one action that's like the golden ticket leading you closer to your number one goal and write it down. And here's the twist: aim to conquer it before noon.

Why the morning rush, you might ask? Because life has a knack for throwing surprises our way. Unexpected meetings, surprise phone calls, or the sudden appearance of your neighbor's cat in your living room—all are potential derailments to your plans. Setting that morning deadline is like putting on your superhero cape; it helps you shield your task from life's curveballs.

And when the day winds down, and you're cozied up in bed, you can enjoy a well-earned slumber knowing that you've made tangible progress on your goals. It's not just a task completed; it's a victory dance under the moonlight, celebrating your journey toward your dreams.

If you've got a little extra time, go ahead and jot down your must-dos and could-dos. The must-dos are your MVPs for the day—the essential appointments, the critical work tasks, and, of course, dinner (cooked or ordered). Keep your priorities in check.

Now let's talk about the could-dos. These are like the cherries on top of your sundae. They're nice-to-haves, but remember, we don't should all over ourselves. We're not imposing unnecessary pressure. Instead, consider them delightful options—tasks you'd love to dive into if the day allows. No pressure, just fun possibilities (and don't forget to ask yourself, "Can any of these tasks be delegated?").

Arrange your tasks in order: start with your number one task, followed by your must-dos, and sprinkle in your could-dos if time and energy permit. And at the end of your victorious day, don't forget to reward yourself! Whether it's a dance party in your living room, a stroll in the park, a cozy moment with your favorite book, or a cocktail on the back porch, take a bow and revel in your accomplishments. You've conquered the day, and you absolutely deserve it!

Own your mama

I know exactly how chaotic and jam-packed your life can be. You juggle a gazillion tasks each day, leaving you sometimes wondering, "Did I truly connect with my kids today?" It's easy to fall into that bedtime trap of wishing you had done more. But what if I told you that I've found a secret to make your days brighter and your connections with your children deeper? It's the incredible power of committing to just one thing each day for or with your little ones. That is what "owning your mama" is about.

This isn't just another item on your never-ending to-do lists. It's a daily dose of pure enchantment, a promise to yourself and your kids that you'll be there—completely and authentically. It's the remedy to those nightly thoughts of "Am I really present in my children's lives?" By choosing just one special thing to do for or with your children each day, you're not just making a commitment; you're sprinkling a little mom magic into your daily routine.

The key here is authenticity. Whatever you choose to do, it needs to feel real—something that genuinely resonates with your family. It could be as straightforward as saying, "Tonight, I'll be fully present with my kids for five minutes. No phones, just us." Or maybe it involves an exciting hands-on activity, like going on a nature walk or diving into a baking-soda-and-vinegar-explosion experiment. After all, you know your kids better than anyone else, so select that one thing that will light up their faces and write it down as your daily promise.

Even on the craziest days when it feels like there just aren't enough hours, I encourage you to take a moment to commit to that one magical thing you'll do with or for your kids. Write it down, embrace it, and make it a cherished part of your daily routine. Motherhood isn't just about surviving; it's about thriving, one magical moment at a time. With our daily dose of mom magic, we're not just shaping our days; we're shaping memories that will last a lifetime.

Yield potential

You've already knocked most of the Grace and Joy routine. Now it's time to live fully in your day. You've chugged water, kicked things off with some intentional movement, even had a moment with yourself. You have taken time to get really clear on what you want for the future and have taken time to feel that positive feeling of gratitude, right now. You're clear on the one thing you need to do today, for you and for your kids.

It's time to show your yield potential. This is a riff on farm talk: it's the maximum growth a crop can achieve when everything's perfect. In our lives, it's all about giving ourselves the best possible head start, nurturing our dreams, and being unstoppable. Completing Grace and Joy does that. So go forth and yield your potential, Mama!

If you can strut into your day with confidence and with the belief that you can tackle anything, you become the sunshine in your own life. You radiate positivity, and guess what? More great days are the result! Following the Grace and Joy routine each morning is your secret sauce for living your dreams.

Cheers to your Grace and Joy!

Here's to you, finding grace and joy each day! With that grace and joy comes the peace and fulfillment you deserve. I'm so happy that you have made it this far in the book and are ready to get out there, delegate, and slay.

Please take a moment to celebrate yourself. You've put in a lot of work and come a long way since opening this book. Pause, take a beat, and recognize your growth—it's worth celebrating. One of my favorite celebratory drinks is sangria. To make traditional sangria you need time; letting it sit is what gives it such great flavor. Still, a lot of times I find myself wanting an impromptu celebration; that's where Quick Sangria comes in. All the flavor and fun with none of the wait. Give this recipe a go and indulge in the sweet, sweet life you are creating.

QUICK SANGRIA

Ingredients

1 cup orange soda (I like Fanta)

1 cup red wine

½ cup frozen mixed fruit (such as berries, peaches, and grapes)

Orange slice, for garnish (optional)

Instructions

1. In a large glass, combine the orange soda and wine. Stir gently to mix the ingredients.
2. Add the frozen mixed fruit. Stir again.
3. Add a few ice cubes to the glass.
4. Optionally, garnish with an orange slice.
5. Drink up and high-five yourself for being awesome.

15

The Next Moment

MAMA, YOU DID IT! I'm so proud of you for taking the time to focus on your needs. I'm thrilled about the difference we'll all see in the world as you begin to flourish through delegating. You'll free yourself up to work on more impactful tasks, like things that move your heart, or maybe even take a break and replenish yourself.

Before you close this book, take a moment to remember where you were when you opened it.

- Were you overwhelmed? Sad? Frustrated? Angry?
- Were you frustrated by the search for work-life balance?
- Did you feel like you had to do it all to be happy?
- Did you worry that you would never be able to show up for your kids because you had too much to do at work?

- Did you worry that you would never be able to advance your career because you had too much going on outside of work?

Whatever challenges and negative feelings you faced before opening this book, my sincere wish is that they have subsided. I hope you are now feeling confident in your ability to delegate, and you know that you don't have to do it all to be happy.

I want to remind you that as you continue down this path of delegating to flourish, you are not the only one who will benefit. Working moms are the backbone of society. We are raising the next generation and helping to grow the economy. When we do better, everyone does better. Our families are happier and healthier, our places of work are more profitable, and our communities are stronger.

Staying consistent with your routine

We all know how important consistency is, and I know how hard it can be to deliver. So let's dive into a few strategies for maintaining your Grace and Joy routine.

- *Prepare for smooth sailing.* Cut down on the morning madness by preparing. Set out a journal you can express your gratitude in every day. Make sure you have water at your bedside so you can wake up and hydrate without much thought. Go to thesavvyworkingmom.com/toolkit to download printouts to help you follow the routine each day.

- *Practice accountability.* Why not make your Grace and Joy morning routine a team effort? Share it with a friend or family member, or team up with a fellow mama. When someone else knows your intentions, it adds an extra layer of accountability to keep you on the right track.

Consistency, not perfection. You're human, and you're allowed to have off days.

- *Celebrate your wins.* At the end of week, do something special for yourself if you've gone through the routine each day.
- *Set visual reminders.* Place visual reminders around your space. Sticky notes on the fridge asking "Are you getting your Grace and Joy?" can be powerful reminders and motivators.
- *Stay flexible and be kind to yourself.* Life is full of surprises, and sometimes our routines get a little shaken up. While ideally you would complete all the steps in the first ninety minutes of your day, the most important thing is that you go through each step every day—even if it's just before bed.
- *Truly give yourself grace.* Consistency, not perfection. Repeat after me: "Consistency over perfection." You're human, and you're allowed to have off days. If you miss a step or two, don't sweat it. Acknowledge it, then get back on the fun morning train.

With these steps, you can follow the Grace and Joy morning routine to energize and excite you. Remember, consistency is the key to success, and adding a pinch of fun makes it all the more delightful. So let's make every morning a Grace and Joy party!

Cheers to consistent delegating!

As you continue to delegate, your life isn't the only one that will improve.

Your taking the time to delegate will also have a positive impact on your family, colleagues, company, and friends. Those you delegate to will have the opportunity to grow.

Those who interact with you will be getting a better version of you, one that is at peace and fulfilled—which provides space for you to be more present, make better decisions, and have more patience.

So cheers to you and all that you don't do!

One of my favorite sayings is, "Everything in moderation, including excess." Because, you know, sometimes we all need a little extra in our lives. And with all the effort you exerted to finish this work and put your delegation plan into play, today is a great day for you to indulge in some excess. One of my favorite excess drinks is Champagne Cocktail. Why? Because it's actual champagne from France, which, by nature, is extravagant, and because it's mixing champagne with other ingredients, which many purists would consider excess.

CHAMPAGNE COCKTAIL

Ingredients

1 sugar cube

2 to 3 dashes Angostura bitters

Champagne (if you really must use sparkling wine, I suggest cava over prosecco)

Lemon peel or cherry, for garnish (optional)

Instructions

1. Place a sugar cube at the bottom of a champagne flute.
2. Add the Angostura bitters onto the sugar cube. The bitters will help to balance the sweetness of the champagne.
3. Slowly pour the champagne into the flute, filling it almost to the top.
4. Gently stir the cocktail to help dissolve the sugar cube and mix the bitters with the champagne.
5. Optionally, garnish the cocktail with a lemon peel or a cherry for added flavor and flair.
6. Serve immediately and visualize yourself flourishing.

Extra, Extra: How to Do It

But wait, there's more! Welcome to the bonus round, a guide to help ensure your success.

Have you ever tried assembling furniture from a manual only to end up with a wobbling piece that looks nothing like the showroom model? And you know things would have been better if you just looked at the picture for inspiration instead of following the instructions? Sometimes, following step-by-step instructions can be more confusing than helpful. The same goes for learning new skills or navigating complex situations. This is why following examples can be a game changer compared to simply reading the rules.

The power of context

Rules and instructions are important; they provide the framework and boundaries within which we operate. However, they often lack the context that makes understanding and applying them easier. When you follow an example, you see the rules in action. You get to understand the nuances, the little tricks, and the common pitfalls, all of which can make a huge difference in achieving the desired outcome.

Think of it this way: reading the rules is like getting a written recipe. Sure, you have all the necessary components and steps, but it can be hard to visualize how to follow them. When the recipe says "vigorously whip," how vigorous is "vigorously"? Examples act as the video for the recipe, showing you how to combine those ingredients to make something great.

The visual learning advantage

Many of us are visual learners. We grasp concepts more effectively when we can see them in action. Watching someone perform a task or walking through a detailed example can make the learning process smoother and more intuitive. This is why video tutorials, step-by-step guides with images, and real-life examples are so popular and effective.

For instance, let's say you're learning to play a musical instrument. Reading about finger placements, chord progressions, and timing can be overwhelming. But watching someone play the instrument, seeing their hand movements, and hearing the music they produce can make it click. Suddenly, the rules make sense because you've seen them applied successfully.

Tried-and-true scripts for easier conversations

One area where examples shine is communication. Whether it's negotiating a salary, resolving a conflict, or delegating a task, conversations can be tricky. You can read all the rules about effective communication, but when it comes time to actually talk, you might freeze up or stumble over your words.

This is where tried-and-true scripts come in handy. Scripts are essentially examples of conversations that have gone successfully in the past. They provide a road map for what to say, how to say it, and when to say it. Using scripts doesn't mean you're being inauthentic; it means you're preparing yourself to communicate more effectively.

For example, if you need to delegate a task to a team member, you might find it difficult to convey all the necessary details and set clear expectations. But if you have a script that outlines exactly how to structure the conversation, what key points to cover, and how to follow up, it suddenly becomes much easier. You're not just winging it—you're following a proven method that increases the likelihood of success.

Building confidence through practice

Following examples also helps build confidence. When you see how something is done and then replicate it, you get immediate feedback on your performance. This practice reinforces learning and builds your confidence in your abilities. Over time, as you become more familiar with the examples and scripts, you'll find that you can adapt them to suit different situations, making you more versatile and effective.

Customizing examples to fit your style

One of the best things about following examples is that you can customize them to fit your personal style and circumstances. Rules are often rigid, but examples can be flexible.

You can tweak and adjust them to better align with your needs and preferences.

For instance, let's go back to the task delegation example. A script may suggest saying, "I need you to complete this task by Friday." But if your team member responds better to a collaborative approach, you might adjust the script to say, "Let's work together to make sure this task is completed by Friday. How can I support you in getting it done?" The essence of the message remains the same, but you've adapted it to better fit your team's dynamics.

The real-world application

The real-world application of rules through examples makes learning more practical and less theoretical. It's one thing to know the theory behind something, but it's another to see it applied successfully in a real-world scenario. Examples bridge the gap between theory and practice, providing a clearer path to mastery.

In conclusion, while rules and instructions are necessary, following examples often makes the learning process easier, more intuitive, and more effective. Tried-and-true scripts can simplify conversations, reduce anxiety, and increase the chances of successful communication. By incorporating examples into your learning and development, you can build confidence, adapt techniques to suit your style, and achieve better outcomes in both personal and professional settings. To that end, I've included this section to get you on your way to more peace and joy quickly.

Grace and Joy schedule examples

The Grace and Joy morning routine isn't just a checklist. It's our daily quest for peace and fulfillment. It's about seizing the day, setting your intentions, and embracing a life full of growth and joy. Stick with this routine, and you'll be the composer and conductor of your life symphony. You'll be clear on where you should be spending your time, which makes it easier to eliminate and delegate. You will live the life of your dreams.

I've put together different schedules to fit whatever time you've got, whether it's six, fourteen, or twenty-seven minutes.

<6 minutes

15 seconds: Drink a cold glass of water.

2 minutes: Stretch.

1 minute: Visualize the life you want.

1 minute: Say out loud the people and things you're grateful for.

1 minute: Write down the most important thing to do that day.

30 seconds: Write down what you will commit to doing with your kids today.

<14 minutes

15 seconds: Drink a cold glass of water.

10 minutes: Move (walk, stretch, run).

1 minute: Visualize the life you want.

1 minute: Say out loud the people and things you're grateful for.

1 minute: Write down the most important thing to do that day.

30 seconds: Write down what you will commit to doing with your kids today.

<27 minutes

15 seconds: Drink a cold glass of water.

15 minutes: Move (walk, stretch, run).

3 minutes: Visualize the life you want.

5 minutes: Write down the people and things you're grateful for.

2 minutes: Write down the most important thing to do that day and visualize completing it.

1 minute: Write down what you will commit to doing with your kids today and visualize it happening.

Benefits of getting hydrated

Here are some of the benefits that come with hydrating.

- *Replenishes your body:* By starting your day with hydration, you're replenishing your body's lost fluids from a night's rest, ensuring you're ready to perform at your best.

- *Boosts metabolism:* Morning hydration kick-starts your metabolism, helping you burn more calories throughout the day, which is great news for your fitness goals.

- *Provides clear complexion:* It's no secret that drinking water flushes out toxins, leading to a healthy and clear complexion. Get ready to greet the day with radiant skin!

- *Enhances cognitive function:* Hydration jump-starts brain function, enhancing mental clarity and concentration, setting you up for success in your daily tasks.

- *Aids digestion:* Morning hydration activates your digestive system, making it easier to process food throughout the day, ensuring you feel comfortable.

- *Supports weight management:* Staying hydrated can curb feelings of hunger, potentially preventing overeating and supporting your weight management goals.
- *Alleviates fatigue:* Dehydration can lead to fatigue, but proper morning hydration helps you feel alert and energized to conquer your day.
- *Provides a healthy glow:* Hydration enhances skin elasticity and radiance, promoting a youthful and confident appearance.
- *Supports a strong immune system:* A well-hydrated body is better equipped to fend off illnesses and infections, keeping you feeling your best.
- *Prevents headaches:* Dehydration can trigger headaches, so morning hydration prevents the likelihood of experiencing them.
- *Regulates body temperature:* Proper hydration helps regulate body temperature, ensuring you stay comfortable throughout the day.
- *Promotes kidney health:* Adequate water intake supports kidney function, flushing out waste and maintaining your kidneys' health.
- *Boosts mood:* Staying hydrated can have a positive impact on your mood, reducing feelings of irritability.
- *Lubricates the joints:* Hydration keeps joints lubricated, potentially reducing the risk of joint pain and stiffness.
- *Aids in heart health:* Proper hydration aids in maintaining healthy blood circulation and heart function.
- *Prevents UTIs:* Drinking water in the morning can help prevent urinary tract infections by flushing out bacteria.

- *Promotes regularity:* Morning hydration can help prevent constipation and support regular bowel movements.
- *Improves nutrient absorption:* Proper hydration improves the body's ability to absorb essential nutrients from food.
- *May prevent muscle cramps:* Dehydration can lead to muscle cramps, but morning hydration may prevent or alleviate them.
- *Sets a positive tone:* Starting your day with a glass of water sets a positive tone for making healthier choices throughout the day.

Benefits of choosing you

There are also numerous benefits to making your first action of the day about choosing yourself.

- *Improved well-being:* Prioritizing self-care sets a positive tone, improving your overall sense of well-being and happiness.
- *Reduced stress:* Self-care activities can reduce stress levels, helping you approach the day with a calm mind.
- *Enhanced resilience:* Engaging in self-care can boost your mental and emotional resilience, making you better equipped to handle challenges.
- *Increased productivity:* Taking time for self-care can improve focus and concentration, leading to increased productivity.
- *Better physical health:* Prioritizing self-care may lead to healthier habits like regular exercise, balanced nutrition, and adequate sleep.

- *Enhanced mental clarity:* Self-care practices can enhance mental clarity, aiding decision-making and problem-solving.
- *Improved relationships:* When you prioritize self-care, you're better able to show up as your best self in your relationships, leading to healthier connections.
- *Enhanced creativity:* Self-care can spark creativity, helping you approach tasks and challenges with fresh perspectives.
- *Increased self-compassion:* Self-care encourages the benefits of self-compassion and self-acceptance, fostering a positive self-image.
- *Balanced emotions:* Engaging in self-care can help regulate emotions, reducing mood swings and promoting emotional stability.
- *Better sleep:* A morning self-care routine can improve sleep quality, helping you wake up refreshed and energized.
- *Strengthened boundaries:* Prioritizing self-care can lead to setting healthier boundaries in both your personal and your professional life.
- *Enhanced problem-solving:* A clear and rested mind from self-care can lead to more effective problem-solving skills.
- *Increased gratitude:* Self-care often includes gratitude practices, helping you appreciate the positive aspects of your life.
- *Greater self-confidence:* Prioritizing self-care can boost self-esteem and self-confidence, helping you tackle challenges with self-assuredness.
- *Improved physical health:* Self-care may lead to better physical health through activities such as exercise, stretching, and healthy eating.

- *Enhanced self-reflection:* Morning self-care allows time for self-reflection, helping you set intentions and goals for the day.

- *Better stress management:* Self-care practices can equip you with stress management tools, reducing the impact of daily stressors.

- *Greater life satisfaction:* Consistent self-care can lead to a greater sense of life satisfaction and fulfillment.

Benefits of reconnecting with your body

Here's what you get when you take a few moments to reconnect with your body.

- *Improved cognitive function:* Sleep often involves a disconnection between your conscious mind and your physical body. Reconnecting these two aspects upon waking helps improve cognitive function. It enhances mental clarity, focus, and alertness for the day ahead. As you embrace the new day, your mind is better prepared to tackle tasks and make decisions with precision.

- *Enhanced mindfulness:* Reconnecting allows you to become more mindful of your body and its sensations. This heightened awareness can lead to better stress management. By paying close attention to your body's signals, you can navigate daily stressors and emotional challenges with greater ease. Mindfulness promotes emotional regulation and an overall sense of well-being.

- *Stress reduction:* Deliberately reconnecting your mind and body in the morning can help reduce stress levels.

Techniques like deep breathing, stretching, or meditating can calm your nervous system. As you engage in these mindful practices, you prepare yourself to face daily stressors with resilience. Stress becomes a manageable force rather than an overwhelming burden.

- *Increased energy levels:* By reestablishing the connection between your mind and body, you activate essential physiological processes. This helps you feel more awake and energized, promoting a positive start to the day. Instead of feeling groggy, you greet the morning with a sense of vitality and enthusiasm.

- *Improved physical health:* Reconnecting allows you to assess your body's physical state, addressing any discomfort or tension. This can lead to better posture, reduced muscle stiffness, and an overall sense of physical well-being. Caring for your body in the morning sets a foundation for physical health throughout the day.

- *Emotional balance:* Reconnecting facilitates emotional balance by enabling you to acknowledge and address any lingering thoughts or emotions from the previous day or night. This emotional awareness can enhance your ability to navigate daily challenges. You can approach situations with a calm and centered mind.

- *Enhanced productivity:* A strong mind-body connection can boost productivity by helping you stay present and engaged in your tasks. This, in turn, can lead to better time management and task execution. With heightened focus and a clear mind, you become more efficient in your endeavors.

- *Strengthened mind-body relationship:* Reconnecting each morning nurtures a positive relationship between your mind and your body. Over time, this can improve your overall health and well-being. You become attuned to your body's signals, allowing for better self-care and healthier habits.

- *Self-care and self-compassion:* Morning rituals that involve reconnecting provide an opportunity for self-care and self-compassion. This self-love and self-acceptance can set a positive tone for the day. You start the morning by nurturing your well-being, fostering a healthy self-image, and acknowledging your worth.

- *Alignment with goals:* Reconnecting helps align your physical and mental states with your goals and intentions for the day. This alignment can enhance your sense of purpose and direction. You step into each day with a clear understanding of what you aim to achieve.

Benefits of accepting the moment

The benefits of this morning silence practice are vast and transformative. Let's explore some of the ways it can positively impact your life.

- *Improved cognitive function:* By reconnecting your mind and body, morning silence enhances cognitive function, sharpening your mental clarity, focus, and alertness for the day's challenges.

- *Stress reduction:* This practice promotes relaxation, reducing stress hormones and enabling a calmer and more composed start to your day.

- *Emotional stability:* Reconnecting fosters emotional stability, empowering you to navigate daily challenges with greater resilience and emotional balance.
- *Enhanced decision-making:* Clarity of mind and reduced stress contribute to better decision-making.
- *Boosted creativity:* Morning silence can spark creativity, offering fresh perspectives and innovative ideas for tasks and challenges.
- *Mindfulness:* Cultivating mindfulness allows you to be fully present and engaged in the moment, leading to a deeper appreciation of life's beauty.
- *Reduced anxiety:* Practicing silence in the morning can alleviate anxiety, promoting a sense of inner peace and tranquility.
- *Better sleep:* Improved sleep quality can result from morning silence, helping you wake up refreshed and energized.
- *Self-reflection:* Taking a moment to reflect provides a precious opportunity that can help you set intentions and goals for the day ahead based on how you are feeling that day.
- *Increased self-awareness:* Sitting in silence enables you to connect with your inner self, fostering self-awareness and self-acceptance.
- *Enhanced relationships:* Greater emotional stability and mindfulness positively impact your interactions with others, fostering healthier relationships.
- *Reduced reactivity:* Morning silence can reduce impulsive reactions to external stimuli, allowing for more measured responses to challenges.

- *Improved physical health:* Stress reduction, improved sleep, and overall well-being can contribute to better physical health.

- *Cultivation of gratitude:* Practicing silence can encourage gratitude, helping you recognize and appreciate the positive aspects of your life.

- *Greater resilience:* Morning silence enhances mental and emotional resilience, empowering you to face adversity with strength and grace.

- *Balanced start:* It sets a balanced and positive tone for the day, improving your outlook and approach to daily tasks.

- *Enhanced productivity:* Improved focus and reduced stress can lead to increased productivity throughout the day.

- *Strengthened mental health:* A regular practice of morning silence contributes to improved mental health and overall well-being.

- *Self-care:* Taking time for morning silence is a form of self-care, promoting self-compassion and self-love.

- *Alignment with values:* This practice aligns your actions with your values and intentions, helping you lead a more purposeful life.

- *Enhanced problem-solving:* A clear and rested mind from morning silence can lead to more effective problem-solving.

- *Greater life satisfaction:* Consistent morning silence can lead to a greater sense of life satisfaction and fulfillment.

- *Spiritual connection:* For some, morning silence fosters a deeper spiritual connection and a profound sense of inner peace.

Benefits of conjuring the future

Now let's dive into the marvelous benefits of morning visualization.

- *Clarity of goals:* Visualization helps you define your goals clearly. It's like a road map for your dreams, making it crystal clear where you want to go.
- *Improved focus:* Regular visualization exercises supercharge your concentration powers. Say goodbye to distractions and hello to supercharged productivity!
- *Increased confidence:* Visualizing your success is like a booster shot of self-confidence. It reminds you that you've got what it takes, spurring you to take action.
- *Stress reduction:* Visualization is your secret weapon for stress busting. It's like a soothing massage for your mind, leaving you cool as a cucumber in stressful situations.
- *Enhanced performance:* Athletes, musicians, and pros swear by visualization. Why? Because mentally rehearsing your moves leads to peak performance in the real deal.
- *Emotional regulation:* Visualizing yourself in a state of calm and composure can help you rein in your emotions. Goodbye, anxiety; hello, emotional balance!
- *Goal achievement:* When you visualize your goals regularly, you're essentially programming your mind for success. It's like a mental dress rehearsal for life's big moments.
- *Positive mindset:* Visualization is like a backstage pass to a positive mindset. It's your all-access ticket to optimism and a can-do attitude.

- *Resilience:* By visualizing yourself conquering challenges and bouncing back from setbacks, you're arming yourself with mental resilience.

- *Enhanced problem-solving:* Visualization often sparks creative problem-solving. It encourages you to explore new solutions to challenges.

- *Increased motivation:* Regularly visualizing your goals and the rewards that come with them is like rocket fuel for your motivation. You'll be unstoppable!

- *Improved self-awareness:* Visualization can deepen your self-awareness by helping you connect with your desires, values, and priorities.

- *Better decision-making:* Visualizing potential outcomes helps you make smarter choices by considering the consequences of your decisions.

- *Enhanced relationships:* Visualizing positive interactions and improved relationships can lead to more harmonious and fulfilling connections with others.

- *Mindfulness:* Visualization is like a mindfulness meditation, urging you to stay present and to savor every delicious moment.

- *Reduction of negative habits:* Visualizing your desired behaviors replaces negative habits with a mental movie of your ideal self.

- *Increased gratitude:* Visualizing your achievements and life's positive aspects enhances feelings of gratitude and contentment.

- *Better sleep:* Incorporating visualization into your bedtime routine leads to more restful nights by soothing your racing mind.

- *Physical health:* Visualization has been linked to better physical health by reducing stress-related ailments and boosting overall well-being.

- *Spiritual connection:* For some, visualization fosters a deeper spiritual connection and a sense of inner peace.

Benefits of expressing gratitude

The benefits of expressing gratitude are extensive and include the following.

- *Improved mental health:* Gratitude is linked to reduced symptoms of depression and anxiety, as it shifts your focus away from negativity and cultivates a positive mindset.

- *Enhanced emotional well-being:* Regularly practicing gratitude leads to increased happiness, contentment, and overall emotional well-being.

- *Stress reduction:* Gratitude practices, such as keeping a gratitude journal, can lower stress levels by promoting relaxation and reducing stress hormones.

- *Better sleep:* Gratitude has been associated with improved sleep quality and duration, calming the mind and reducing bedtime anxiety.

- *Increased resilience:* Gratitude enhances your ability to cope with challenges and adversity, fostering a positive outlook.

- *Stronger relationships:* Expressing gratitude strengthens bonds and deepens connections with others, improving the quality of interactions.

- *Greater life satisfaction:* Gratitude practices contribute to an increased sense of life satisfaction and fulfillment, helping you appreciate life's positives.

- *Improved physical health:* Gratitude is linked to better physical health, including reduced inflammation, lower blood pressure, and a stronger immune system.

- *Enhanced self-esteem:* Grateful individuals tend to have higher self-esteem and self-worth, which boosts their self-confidence.

- *Positive behavior change:* Practicing gratitude can lead to positive changes in behavior, such as adopting healthier habits and reducing negative ones.

- *Increased generosity:* Grateful people are more likely to engage in acts of kindness and generosity, spreading positivity to others.

- *Improved decision-making:* Gratitude encourages thoughtful and deliberate decision-making by considering both positive and negative consequences.

- *Enhanced mindfulness:* Gratitude practices foster mindfulness by encouraging you to be fully present and appreciative of the current moment.

- *Elevated mood:* Expressing gratitude elevates your mood and reduces feelings of irritability and anger.

- *Greater optimism:* Gratitude promotes a more optimistic outlook on life, helping you see opportunities and silver linings in challenging situations.

- *Better social relationships:* Grateful individuals tend to be more empathetic, compassionate, and forgiving, contributing to healthier social interactions.

- *Reduction in materialism:* Gratitude shifts your focus away from material possessions and the pursuit of wealth, leading to a more fulfilling and balanced life.

- *Improved work relationships:* Expressing gratitude at work strengthens team cohesion and enhances workplace relationships, creating a positive work environment.

- *Enhanced coping skills:* Gratitude practices improve your ability to cope with trauma or difficult life events by emphasizing the positives and fostering hope.

- *Spiritual connection:* For some, gratitude deepens their spiritual connection and sense of purpose in life.

Benefits of just picking one

Here are the fantastic benefits of embracing this one-task-wonder approach with a dash of fun.

- *Focus:* Imagine putting on your superhero goggles and sharpening your focus laser-beam style. No more distractions, just you and your task, like a rock star onstage.

- *Clarity:* It's like having a treasure map for your day. You know exactly where X marks the spot—the one task that'll lead you to the treasure chest of your goals.

- *Efficiency:* Picture yourself soaring through tasks like a pro, finishing them faster and better than ever before.

- **Sense of achievement:** Conquering your daily task is like leveling up in your favorite video game. You feel like you're on top of the world, and that's an excellent mood booster!
- **Reduced stress:** A simplified to-do list is like a soothing spa day for your mind. No more fretting over a never-ending list; just one task, one goal at a time.
- **Prioritization:** It's like having a personal assistant that whispers in your ear, "This one's the MVP today!" It helps you sort your tasks by importance and impact.
- **Time management:** Imagine having the power of the Time Stone from *Doctor Strange*. Prioritization ensures you've got enough time for what matters most.
- **Consistency:** Like a daily dose of vitamins, this practice ensures you're making steady progress toward your dreams, one day at a time.
- **Improved decision-making:** It's like having a compass pointing north. Choosing your daily task encourages you to make thoughtful decisions about your day.
- **Better balance:** A well-balanced life is like a delicious recipe. Prioritizing tasks ensures you don't over-sprinkle the work spices in your life dish.
- **Less overwhelm:** Juggling fewer balls in the air is like mastering a juggling act. Say goodbye to the overwhelm of multitasking.
- **Increased creativity:** Immersing yourself in one task is like diving into a sea of ideas. Creativity flows when you have the time to explore it.
- **Enhanced quality:** Imagine turning in a masterpiece every day, like an artist showcasing their finest work.

- *Higher satisfaction:* Completing your daily task is like reaching the finish line of a marathon. You feel on top of the world.

- *Time for self-care:* It's like having a nap on your calendar. Prioritizing one task leaves more room for self-pampering and relaxation.

- *Greater accountability:* Like a personal coach would, it ensures you're staying accountable and making progress.

- *Progress toward goals:* Imagine taking one step closer to your dream every single day. It's like climbing a ladder to success.

- *Reduced procrastination:* No more procrastination monsters under your bed. Prioritization kicks them out and boosts your motivation.

- *Improved relationships:* Picture having more time to laugh, chat, and connect with loved ones. Relationships blossom when you're present.

- *Enhanced memory:* Focusing on one task sharpens your memory. It's like a mental workout for your brain.

- *Increased confidence:* Each completed task is a boost to your confidence. You're on fire, and you know it!

Benefits of owning your mama

The rewards of this daily dose of mom magic are absolutely incredible.

- *Quality time:* Those focused moments create lasting memories and tighten your bonds with your kids.

- *Improved communication:* One-on-one interactions lead to open conversations and a better understanding of your children's thoughts and feelings.

- *Enhanced parent-child relationship:* Engaging in an activity together builds trust and strengthens your unique relationship.

- *Emotional connection:* Focusing on that one activity fosters an emotional connection and empathy, helping you grasp your children's emotions better.

- *Increased attention:* Your kids get your full attention, making them feel incredibly valued.

- *Skills development:* Fun activities help your children develop new skills, interests, and talents.

- *Positive influence:* Being there sets you as a positive role model and shapes your children's values and behavior.

- *Strengthened family bond:* A daily bonding activity brings your family closer together.

- *Stress relief:* Spending quality time with your kids acts as a stress reliever, improving your overall well-being.

- *Better understanding:* You gain insights into your children's interests, strengths, and challenges, helping to support their growth.

- *Improved behavior:* Regular one-on-one time can lead to improved behavior as your children feel secure and understood.

- *Confidence boost:* Quality interactions boost your children's self-esteem and confidence.

- *Enhanced creativity:* Creative activities spark imagination and creativity in both you and your children.
- *Building traditions:* Daily rituals create unique family traditions and special routines.
- *Greater appreciation:* Taking time for daily activities allows us to cherish the small joys of parenthood.
- *Better problem-solving:* Conversations during these activities provide opportunities to address concerns or issues.
- *Positive memories:* Regular shared experiences create a treasure trove of heartwarming memories.
- *Lifelong connection:* Daily interactions pave the way for a lifelong connection with our children.
- *Stress buster:* Spending quality moments with your kids can be a great stress buster, offering relaxation and rejuvenation.
- *Joy and happiness:* Fun-filled activities bring joy and happiness to both you and your little ones.

Delegation equation examples

Example 1: Budget management

Task: Creating and managing the budget, takes approximately two hours per week, fifty-two times a year.

Teaching time: Teaching someone to manage the budget may take four hours initially.

Outcomes review: Reviewing the budget and financial statements with the delegated person may take one hour per month, totaling twelve hours per year.

Equation:
(T)ime: 2 hours per week
(N)umber of times: 52 times per year
(R)equired time to teach: 4 hours
(O)utcomes review: 12 hours per year

Result: (2 × 52) > (4 + 12) = 104 > 16. Delegation recommended.

Example 2: Grocery shopping
Task: Shopping for groceries takes about one hour per week, fifty-two times a year.

Teaching time: Teaching someone how to plan and shop efficiently may take two hours initially.

Outcomes review: Reviewing the shopping list and expenses with the delegated person may take thirty minutes per week, totaling twenty-six hours per year.

Equation:
T: 1 hour per week
N: 52 times per year
R: 2 hours
O: 26 hours per year

Result: (1 × 52) > (2 + 26) = 52 > 28. Delegation recommended.

Example 3: Home maintenance
Task: Monthly home maintenance tasks, such as lawn care and cleaning, take about three hours per week, fifty-two times a year.

Teaching time: Teaching someone how to perform these tasks may take six hours initially.

Outcomes review: Reviewing completed tasks and ensuring quality may take one hour per month, totaling twelve hours per year.

Equation:
T: 3 hours per week
N: 52 times per year
R: 6 hours
O: 12 hours per year

Result: (3 × 52) > (6 + 12) = 156 > 18. Delegation recommended.

Example 4: Social media management for a business

Task: Managing social media accounts for a business takes about five hours per week, fifty-two times a year.

Teaching time: Teaching someone how to curate content, schedule posts, and engage with followers may take eight hours initially.

Outcomes review: Reviewing social media performance and engagement metrics may take two hours per week, totaling 104 hours per year.

Equation:
T: 5 hours per week
N: 52 times per year
R: 8 hours
O: 104 hours per year

Result: (5 × 52) > (8 + 104) = 260 > 112. Delegation recommended.

Example 5: Family event planning

Task: Planning and organizing family events, such as birthdays and holidays, takes about ten hours per event, with four events per year.

Teaching time: Teaching someone how to plan and coordinate events may take twelve hours initially.

Outcomes review: Reviewing event plans, budgets, and attendee feedback may take three hours per event, totaling twelve hours per year.

Equation:
T: 10 hours per event
N: 4 times per year
R: 12 hours
O: 12 hours per year

Result: (10 × 4) > (12 + 12) = 40 > 24. Delegation recommended.

Example 6: Data entry and analysis for a small business
Task: Entering and analyzing sales data for a small business takes approximately two hours per week, fifty-two times a year.

Teaching time: Teaching someone how to input and analyze data using relevant software may take three hours initially.

Outcomes review: Reviewing data accuracy and insights with the delegated person may take one hour per week, totaling fifty-two hours per year.

Equation:
T: 2 hours per week
N: 52 times per year
R: 3 hours
O: 52 hours per year

Result: (2 × 52) > (3 + 52) = 104 > 55. Delegation recommended.

Example 7: Home cooking and meal preparation
Task: Cooking and meal preparation for a family takes about eight hours per week, fifty-two times a year.

Teaching time: Teaching someone how to plan meals, prepare ingredients, and cook may take six hours initially.

Outcomes review: Reviewing meal plans and ensuring dietary preferences are met may take one hour per week, totaling fifty-two hours per year.

Equation:
T: 8 hours per week
N: 52 times per year
R: 6 hours
O: 52 hours per year
Result: (8 × 52) > (6 + 52) = 416 > 58. Delegation recommended.

Example 8: Event planning for a community group

Task: Planning and coordinating events for a community group takes about six hours per event, with eight events per year.

Teaching time: Teaching someone how to organize events, manage logistics, and communicate with participants may take four hours initially.

Outcomes review: Reviewing event feedback, attendance numbers, and budget reports may take one hour per event, totaling eight hours per year.

Equation:
T: 6 hours per event
N: 8 times per year
R: 4 hours
O: 8 hours per year
Result: (6 × 8) > (4 + 8) = 48 > 12. Delegation recommended.

Example 9: Garden maintenance

Task: Maintaining a home garden, including planting, watering, and weeding, takes about three hours per week, fifty-two times a year.

Teaching time: Teaching someone how to care for different plants, identify pests, and maintain soil health may take five hours initially.

Outcomes review: Reviewing garden health and addressing any issues may take one hour per week, totaling fifty-two hours per year.

Equation:
T: 3 hours per week
N: 52 times per year
R: 5 hours
O: 52 hours per year

Result: (3 × 52) > (5 + 52) = 156 > 57. Delegation recommended.

Example 10: Bookkeeping for personal finances

Task: Managing personal finances and bookkeeping, including budgeting, tracking expenses, and reconciling accounts, takes about four hours per month, twelve times a year.

Teaching time: Teaching someone how to use financial software, categorize transactions, and balance accounts may take three hours initially.

Outcomes review: Reviewing financial reports, budget adherence, and investment performance may take one hour per month, totaling twelve hours per year.

Equation:
T: 4 hours per month
N: 12 times per year
R: 3 hours
O: 12 hours per year

Result: (4 × 12) > (3 + 12) = 48 > 15. Delegation recommended.

Delegation script examples and templates

Feel free to adjust any details to better fit your voice and context!

Q4 financial report delegation script
Here is a sample script for delegating to someone at work.

Introduction
Hi Jane, I hope you're doing well. We are here to discuss an important task I need to delegate to you, and I want to provide all the necessary details to ensure it's completed successfully.

Task description
The task I need you to work on is the Q4 financial report. Specifically, you will be responsible for compiling, analyzing, and presenting the financial data for the fourth quarter.

Expectations
To ensure the task is completed to the required standard, here are the key expectations.

- Objective: The primary objective of this task is to provide a comprehensive overview of the company's financial performance in Q4.

- Deliverables: The deliverables for this task include a detailed report with monthly, weekly, and daily breakdowns by customer type.

- Quality standards: The report should be accurate, well-organized, and formatted according to the company's reporting guidelines.

Deadlines

The deadlines for this task are as follows.

1. Initial draft/progress report: April 15
2. Review meeting: April 22
3. Final submission: May 7

Resources

You can access the following resources to help you complete the task:

- Previous financial reports
- Financial analysis software
- Company data archives

Support

If you have any questions or need further assistance, please don't hesitate to reach out. I'm here to support you and ensure you have everything you need to succeed.

Follow-up

We will have a follow-up meeting on April 22 to review the progress and address any challenges you may be facing. Please ensure you are ready to discuss your progress by then.

Closing

Thank you for taking on this task. I'm confident in your ability to complete it successfully. Let's touch base soon to ensure everything is on track.

Household chore delegation script

Here is a sample script for delegating a household chore to your partner that clearly communicates the task, expectations, and deadlines.

Introduction
Hey, babe, I want to discuss a household chore that I need your support with and to provide all the necessary details to ensure it's completed successfully.

Task description
The chore I need your support with is cleaning the kitchen. Specifically, you will be responsible for wiping down the counters, washing the dishes, and sweeping the floor.

Expectations
To ensure the chore is completed to the required standard, here are the key expectations.

- Objective: The primary objective of this chore is to maintain a clean and hygienic kitchen.
- Steps: The steps involved include the following.
- Wipe down all countertops and surfaces.
- Wash and dry all dishes.
- Sweep the kitchen floor.
- Quality standards: The counters should be free of crumbs and stains, all dishes should be clean and put away, and the floor should be free of debris.

Deadlines
The deadlines for this chore are as follows.
1. Start time: After dinner tonight
2. Completion time: Before we go to bed

Resources
You can access the following resources to help you complete the chore:

1. Cleaning supplies (spray, cloths)
2. Dish soap and sponge
3. Broom and dustpan

Support
If you have any questions or need further assistance, please let me know. I'm here to support you and ensure you have everything you need to succeed. I appreciate you.

Follow-up
We can check in before our son's bath time to review the progress and make sure everything is on track.

Closing
Thank you for taking on this chore. I really appreciate you doing your part in keeping our home running smoothly.

Household chore delegation template
Here's a template so you can plan.

Introduction
Hey, [husband's pet name], I want to discuss a household chore that I need your support with and to provide all the necessary details to ensure it's completed successfully.

Task description
The chore I need your support with is [briefly describe the chore]. Specifically, you will be responsible for [provide a detailed description of what the chore entails].

Expectations
To ensure the chore is completed to the required standard, here are the key expectations.

- Objective: The primary objective of this chore is [explain the main goal or purpose].
- Steps: The steps involved in this chore include [list the specific steps or actions needed].
- Quality standards: The quality standards to be maintained are [mention any specific quality criteria or standards that need to be met].

Deadlines
The deadlines for this chore are as follows.
1. Start time: [when you want the chore to start]
2. Completion time: [when you want the chore to be finished by]

Resources
You can access the following resources to help you complete the chore:
1. [Resource 1]
2. [Resource 2]
3. [Resource 3]

Support
If you have any questions or need further assistance, please let me know. I'm here to support you and ensure you have everything you need to succeed. I appreciate you.

Follow-up
We can check in on [date/time] to review the progress and make sure everything is on track.

Closing
Thank you for taking on this chore. I really appreciate you doing your part in keeping our home running smoothly. Let's touch base soon to ensure everything is on track.

Delegation script example for child doing a household chore

Introduction
Hey, Emma, I need your help with an important household chore. Would you be able to take care of the laundry this week?

Task description
Specifically, you will be responsible for sorting the clothes, washing them, drying them, and putting them away.

Expectations
To ensure the laundry is done properly, here are the key expectations.

- Objective: The main goal is to make sure all our clothes are clean and neatly put away.

- Steps: The steps involved include the following.
  - Sort the clothes by color (lights, darks, and whites).
  - Load the washing machine with one type of sorted clothes.
  - Add the right amount of detergent.
  - Set the washing machine to the appropriate cycle and start it.
  - Move the washed clothes to the dryer.
  - Set the dryer to the appropriate cycle and start it.
  - Fold the dry clothes and put them away.

- Quality standards:
  - Clothes are folded.
  - Clothes are put into the designated areas.

Deadlines
The deadlines for this chore are as follows.

1. Start time: Today after school
2. Completion time: By the end of the day

Resources
You can access the following resources to help you complete the laundry:

1. Laundry detergent (located on the shelf above the washing machine)
2. Washing machine and dryer (instructions are on the machines)
3. Laundry baskets for sorting and transporting clothes

Support
If you have any questions or need further assistance, please ask me. I'm here to help you and ensure you have everything you need to do a great job.

Follow-up
We can check in tonight before you start to get ready for bed to review how it went and see if you need any help.

Closing
Thank you for helping with the laundry. I really appreciate your effort in keeping our home clean and organized.

Delegation template for child doing a household chore

Introduction
Hey, [child's name], I need your help with an important household chore.

Task description
The chore I need you to handle is [name the chore]. Specifically, you will be responsible for [provide a detailed description of what the chore entails].

Expectations
To ensure the [chore] is done properly, here are the key expectations.

- Objective: The main goal of this chore is [explain the main goal or purpose].
- Steps: The steps involved in this chore include [list the specific steps or actions needed].
- Quality standards: The quality standards to be maintained are [mention any specific quality criteria or standards that need to be met].

Deadlines
The deadlines for this chore are as follows.
1. Start time: [when you want the chore to start]
2. Completion time: [when you want the chore to be finished by]

Resources
You can access the following resources to help you complete the chore:
1. [Resource 1]
2. [Resource 2]
3. [Resource 3]

Support
If you have any questions or need further assistance, please let me know. I'm here to help you and ensure you have everything you need to do a great job.

Follow-up
We can check in on [date/time] to review how it went and see if you need any help.

Closing
Thank you for helping out. I really appreciate your effort in keeping our home clean and organized.

Acknowledgments

THIS BOOK would not have been possible without the incredible support of—and inspiration from—so many people in my life.

First and foremost, I want to thank the number one working mom in my life, my mom, Linda. You set the foundation upon which I've built my life, teaching me the value of hard work, resilience, and love. To my amazing grandmother, your wisdom has guided me through every job, degree, and act of kindness. Thank you for encouraging me to plan, dream big, and strive for greatness.

A heartfelt thank you to my aunt Tante Tante for helping turn my creative visions into realities. Your unwavering belief in me has brought so many of my dreams to life. To my mother-in-law, thank you for being my constant cheerleader, always lifting me up with your words of encouragement.

To my husband, thanks, babe, for standing by my side and supporting me through every step of this journey. You make everything possible. To all the extraordinary women in my family, thank you for giving me the courage to be brave, to take risks, and to never back down from a challenge.

To my kids, you are my greatest inspiration. You push me to stretch and grow in ways I never thought possible, and for that, I am endlessly grateful.

A special thank you to my coaching clients—your trust in me fuels my passion for helping others. To the event managers who have given me the opportunity to speak to their audiences, thank you for allowing me to share my message with the world.

This book reflects all the love, support, and encouragement I have received from each of you. I am forever grateful.

PHOTO: JODY SMITH

About the Author

SPEAKER, PODCASTER, AND FOUNDER of The Savvy Working Mom, Whitnee Hawthorne is a mama to two littles and a versatile executive with significant contributions to both Fortune 500 companies and start-ups. But if you ask which role has brought her the most fulfillment, it's the role of advocating for breadwinning mamas.

Through her workshops, podcast, TEDx talk, and coaching programs, she provides actionable, real-world steps that empower breadwinning mamas to immediately enhance their productivity, boost their confidence, and inject more joy into their lives.

When Hawthorne is not coaching and speaking, she is trying new recipes, hanging out with her boys, or sipping a Manhattan on the front porch. You can connect with her at @thesavvyworkingmom on all social channels.

Finding peace, joy, and fulfillment at work and at home isn't about doing it all.

It's about knowing what truly matters to you, prioritizing those things, and mastering the art of delegation. As the symphony of our lives plays, the journey can sometimes still feel overwhelming, so I want you to know I'm here to support you.

Listen to my podcast
The Savvy Working Mom podcast is your go-to resource for tips, strategies, and inspiration to help you thrive in both your personal and professional life. Join me as I share key insights from my experience as an executive, coach, and working mom, along with interviews with other amazing women who are balancing it all. Tune in on your favorite platform here: thesavvyworkingmom.com/podcast.

Access free tools for working moms
At The Savvy Working Mom, I've created a collection of free resources designed to help you reclaim your time, reduce overwhelm, and achieve your goals. Whether you're looking for strategies on time management, delegation, or self-care, these tools are here to support you every step of the way. Access them here: thesavvyworkingmom.com/resource-library.

Get my newsletter

If you've enjoyed the insights shared here, you'll love receiving my monthly newsletter. Sign up at thesavvyworkingmom.com/toolkit to get exclusive tips, personal stories, and actionable advice delivered straight to your inbox. It's all about helping you navigate life as a savvy working mom, one empowering step at a time.

Invite me to speak

Onstage, I speak from the heart, empowering women to embrace their strengths, delegate with confidence, and create lives filled with joy and fulfillment. My talks inspire career-minded women to take charge of their careers and their lives. If you'd like to book me for a speaking engagement, please contact me here: thesavvyworkingmom.com/speaking.

Share your thoughts

I'd love to hear how my book has impacted your life. If you think it could help other working moms, please consider leaving a positive review on your favorite retail website or online forum. Your feedback not only helps spread the word but also supports other women on their journey to thriving.

Connect with me every day

Let's keep the conversation going! I'm here to answer your questions, share insights, and connect with you on your journey as a savvy working mom. You can find me online—let's connect!

linkedin.com/company/the-savvy-working-mom
@thesavvyworkingmom